"How can we let the Lord use our pain and distresses to bless our lives? Linda Dillow shows us how, sharing rich treasures from the Psalms and from her own life. See afresh how sufficient the Lord is, even in the worst of circumstances."

— RUTH MYERS, author of *Christ Life*; *31 Days of Praise*; *The Perfect Love*; and *The Satisfied Heart*

"Linda Dillow's heart finds rest and strength in secret and holy places. Once again she brings clarity to the human experience and wisely points us to the true Helper."

— GAYLE HAGGARD, director of women's ministries, New Life Church, Colorado Springs, Colorado

A Deeper Kind *of* Calm

Steadfast Faith in the Midst of Adversity

formerly The Blessing Book

LINDA DILLOW

NAVPRESS®

BRINGING TRUTH TO LIFE

The Navigators is an international Christian organization. Our mission is to advance the gospel of Jesus and His kingdom into the nations through spiritual generations of laborers living and discipling among the lost. We see a vital movement of the gospel, fueled by prevailing prayer, flowing freely through relational networks and out into the nations where workers for the kingdom are next door to everywhere.

NavPress is the publishing ministry of The Navigators. The mission of NavPress is to reach, disciple, and equip people to know Christ and make Him known by publishing life-related materials that are biblically rooted and culturally relevant. Our vision is to stimulate spiritual transformation through every product we publish.

© 2003, 2006 by Linda Dillow

All rights reserved. No part of this publication may be reproduced in any form without written permission from NavPress, P.O. Box 35001, Colorado Springs, CO 80935.
www.navpress.com

NAVPRESS, BRINGING TRUTH TO LIFE, and the NAVPRESS logo are registered trademarks of NavPress. Absence of ® in connection with marks of NavPress or other parties does not indicate an absence of registration of those marks.

ISBN 1-60006-075-7

Cover illustration by Getty Images/The Bridgeman Art Library
Creative Team: Dan Rich, Liz Heaney, Darla Hightower, Arvid Wallen, Laura Spray

This book was previously published as *The Blessing Book*, copyright © 2003 by Linda Dillow, published by NavPress.

Some of the anecdotal illustrations in this book are true to life and are included with the permission of the persons involved. All other illustrations are composites of real situations, and any resemblance to people living or dead is coincidental.

Unless otherwise identified, all Scripture quotations in this publication are taken from the HOLY BIBLE: NEW INTERNATIONAL VERSION® (NIV®). Copyright © 1973, 1978, 1984 by International Bible Society. Used by permission of Zondervan Publishing House. All rights reserved. Other versions used include: the New American Standard Bible (NASB), © The Lockman Foundation 1960, 1962, 1963, 1968, 1971, 1972, 1973, 1975, 1977, 1995; THE MESSAGE (MSG). Copyright © 1993, 1994, 1995, 1996, 2000, 2001, 2002. Used by permission of NavPress Publishing Group; the Holy Bible, New Living Translation (NLT), copyright © 1996. Used by permission of Tyndale House Publishers, Inc., Wheaton, Illinois 60189. All rights reserved.

Library of Congress Cataloging-in-Publication Data
Dillow, Linda.
 [Blessing book]
 A deeper kind of calm : steadfast faith in the midst of adversity / Linda Dillow.
 p. cm.
 Previously published as: The blessing book.
 Includes bibliographical references.
 ISBN 1-60006-075-7
 1. Suffering--Religious aspects--Christianity. 2. Consolation.
 I. Title.
 BV4909.D48 2006
 248.8'6--dc22
 2006016326

Printed in the United States of America

1 2 3 4 5 6 / 10 09 08 07 06

FOR A FREE CATALOG OF
NAVPRESS BOOKS & BIBLE STUDIES,
CALL 1-800-366-7788 (USA)
OR 1-800-839-4769 (CANADA)

To Becky, Donna, and Nanci:
I have watched you walk through the Valley of Weeping
with grace and eyes lifted to God.

Contents

Acknowledgments

A big thank-you to:

Liz Heaney: my "super editor" and friend. I continue to learn so much from you.

Lorraine Pintus: the "coauthor" of everything I write. You always find ALL the rocks.

Dan Rich, Terry Behimer, and their team at NavPress: It is a joy and privilege to work with you.

Chapter One

My Valley *of* Weeping

As I hung up the phone, all I could do was weep. This was the sixth phone call I'd received that week from a distraught woman who had shared with me her heartache, leaving my heart broken as well. Their anguish-filled words echoed in my mind:

- "My husband is having an affair with my best friend."
- "I just found drugs in my son's room."
- "I lost my job—what am I going to do?"
- "My breast cancer has returned."

So many hurting women; so many heavy, heavy burdens. I cried out to God: "Is there no end to the pain in this world? O God, give hope to the brokenhearted . . . wrap Your arms of comfort around my friends."

But as I lifted each name to the throne of grace, I added my name to the list.

If God had given me the opportunity to script my story, I'd have written something like *It's a Wonderful Life*. I'd be the light-hearted heroine traipsing through town, seeking opportunities to bless others.

Oh, yes, I'd have a wonderful life—and so would everyone else.

The last three years of my life have looked more like scenes from *Les Misérables* than from *It's a Wonderful Life*. I have had struggles on every front: my relationships, my ministry, my home, and my health. While I can laugh at some of these incidents now, at the time I did not find them particularly amusing! See if you don't agree.

SCENE 1

My husband, Jody, and I took our Polish houseguests for a Wild West adventure to the Flying W Ranch, where we enjoyed a barbecue and western music. When we returned home, our friends entered the house first. When they walked into the kitchen they yelled, "Linda, come quick! Something is wrong." As I rushed in, I discovered that *wrong* did not begin to describe the condition of my kitchen. *Disaster* was a better word.

- A mangled screen lay in the sink.
- Jagged pieces of the pantry doorframe cluttered the floor.
- A kitchen cabinet door covered with splotchy, red marks dangled from one hinge.
- Large, bloody-looking prints covered the stovetop, floor, and countertops.
- Peanut butter jars littered the counter — all of them empty.
- A chunky, brown substance that looked like vomit coated the counter and walls.

A bear had come calling. A very desperate bear. Our house had been closed and locked, except for the window over the kitchen sink, which we'd left open six inches for ventilation. Because the window had a twelve-foot drop-off, we thought our house would be secure, but a ravenous bear would not be dissuaded. Climbing on top of the grill on our deck, he lunged toward the window, heaved his large frame up on the sill, and then smashed through the screen into food heaven. According to neighbors, our ninety-pound dog, Barney, barked incessantly and then stopped abruptly. Apparently the bear had swatted him to silence, leaving a chunk of Barney fur on the floor in the process.

As we cleaned up the mess, we discovered that the blood-like prints on the counters had resulted from the bear breaking a large glass jar of salsa. (Was he a Mexican bear?) The vomitlike muck turned out to be a mixture of baking chocolate and salsa. (A Mexican bear with PMS?) When we finished cleaning up, we went to bed, unaware that our intruder was ready for another try at the Dillow Diner. Once again, he climbed on the grill, lunging for the now-closed window. Hitting it hard, he fell helplessly onto the rocks below. We know this because our houseguests happened to be looking out the window at the time. They are now firmly convinced that the Wild West still exists!

Although our trusty dog needed a pet psychiatrist to recover from the trauma, we were not harmed. The wildlife association said our homeowner's insurance would cover the cost of repairs to our kitchen. Our insurance company said the wildlife association would cover it. They were both wrong. Months later the Dillow bank account coughed up the money.

My plan: Come home to my wonderful, clean house and relax with our guests.

My portion: Clean up a gruesome salsa mess and live for months with jagged door frames and open cabinets while hassling over "who pays" for bear break-ins.

Scene 2

I could hardly wait. My daughter Robin and granddaughter Sofia were coming to visit us from Finland. It had been months since I'd seen either of them, and I anticipated the fun we'd have. Visions danced in my head of trips to the zoo, the park, and of

Sofia and me laughing together. I told Robin to bring something to wear besides jeans. I had made reservations for lunch and then tea at a castle. Afterward we were going shopping!

When Robin and Sofia finally arrived at our home, illness dashed my dreams. Instead of going on shopping trips together, my daughter and I took turns holding and rocking a sick Sofia. Instead of enjoying a leisurely lunch together in a lovely restaurant and tea in a castle, we were dressed in sweats, seated in the kitchen, enticing a feverish toddler with finger foods. This trip was Robin's thirtieth-birthday present. I had plans for fun — instead we had real life.

Then on Saturday Jody casually mentioned that he had passed out while lying on the bed watching TV. When I questioned him further, he said he had passed out several times that week, but he hadn't said anything because he thought "it was no big deal." (After thirty-nine years of marriage, I am no closer to understanding the male species than I was as a bride.)

After convincing this man I love that it WAS a big deal, we drove to the emergency room. The twenty-four-hour EKG they attached to Jody showed that his heart was periodically stopping and his pulse rate was below thirty. While Robin rocked Sofia at home alone, I waited for the surgeon to put a pacemaker in my husband's chest. The surgeon's comment: "This is so serious that I won't let your husband go one night without a pacemaker." Right. No big deal.

My plan: Tea in a castle and zoo-time with Sofia.

My portion: A husband with flat lines on his EKG, a sick Sofia, and an exhausted daughter.

SCENE 3

I had compiled a long list of favorite outdoor activities for the glorious Colorado summer . . . hikes up Raspberry Mountain to my waterfall, barbecues on our deck, and worship times in my "rock sanctuary." Oh, it sounded so wonderful. But it was not to be.

That summer Colorado faced its worst drought in 230 years and the largest fire in its history (the Hayman fire). Flames gobbled up more than 110,000 acres of national forest, polluting our crisp mountain air with toxic smoke and covering our back deck in ash.

Every night I watched the news as firefighters from all over the country told about their rigorous efforts to contain the out-of-control blaze. Planes and helicopters buzzed above the smoke, dumping flame-retardant chemicals on the inferno, but it was like trying to douse a bonfire with water from a thimble.

One afternoon as the fire moved closer to our home at the foothills of the Rockies, the dreaded announcement came: "Be ready to evacuate. Unless the winds change, the fire will be here at midnight."

I scurried through the house gathering pictures and almost forty years of treasures we'd collected from around the world as a result of our years as missionaries: pine furniture from Austria, carpets from China, irreplaceable gifts from special friends, and mementos from our children. Valuable files and documents filled our two offices plus thousands of books, each one a treasure. As the truck with our cherished possessions left our driveway, I watched it join a caravan of cars. Many of our neighbors also were transporting their belongings to a safe place.

Throughout the night I begged God to shift the winds and spare our mountain home. God heard—and He answered. The winds shifted. Although we remained on "standby to evacuate," our neighborhood breathed a sigh of relief. A week later we rejoiced as the official news was given: the danger was over; the Hayman fire was contained.

Have I unpacked all the boxes and put everything back in its place? No. You ask, "Linda, how could you let boxes sit around for four months?" One word: *migraines*. For months I have had a migraine headache almost every day, the latest of the wars I've fought with my hormones. When I have a migraine my vision clouds, my stomach lurches, and my head feels like someone hit it with a two-by-four.

Day after day, I lay in bed with a damp cloth on my forehead. Summer turned into fall. The snap of the first frost shocked Colorado into winter hibernation, turning the life-bearing green leaves to brown. I looked at the gnarled, dead-looking bush outside my window and knew exactly how it must feel.

My plan: A quiet, restful summer.

My portion: A fire-filled, migraine-filled summer.

Over the last three years my portion has also included two surgeries that were supposed to help my body. One failed miserably; the other caused my hormones to go berserk. My tears have wet the carpet as I've grieved over a conflict with someone close to me. Hardest of all, my wonderful husband and I have walked through difficult waters in our marriage. I had always assumed that as we "grew older" our intimacy would grow sweeter. It has . . . but the sweet fragrance has come as the flowers of our love have been tightly pressed.

What has been happening in your life?

Perhaps as you read these scenes from my life, you thought, *Linda had it easy. She hasn't begun to feel the pain I've felt!* And you are right. But pain is pain, and all pain hurts. I've walked with friends whose marriages have been torn asunder by infidelity, pornography, and deceit. I know homes divided by a yellow emotional line. I've grieved with those who have lost a spouse or a child. I've cried with others who spend twenty-four hours every day in chronic pain, death crouching around the corner. I've ached with friends whose children have been diagnosed as autistic, others whose teenagers have wandered far from their Christian faith and embraced drugs, abortions, and "whatever." I've agonized with precious women who live with the horror of sexual abuse . . . evil done to them and to their children. Long is the list of pain: cancer, financial disaster, unemployment, parents with Alzheimer's. What is a bear or a fire in comparison?

Each of us has our own "Valley of Weeping." For some, the valley is shallow. For others, the valley is so deep there seems to be no way out. My own valleys are not anything special . . . they are simply what I have experienced. What do we do when pain overtakes the path of delight we had planned?

People react differently to pain. Many women I know "stuff" their pain by denying its existence or by numbing it with pleasure (alcohol, drugs, shopping, romance novels, television, and so on). Others talk incessantly about it in an attempt to exorcise it. None of these responses brings about the true relief we desire, nor do they glorify God.

God has a different answer for pain. His answer is found in the Psalms.

Most people know the Psalms as God's hymnal of praise, but they are also His picture book of pain. In the Psalms we see anguishing pain poured forth with wrenching honesty and vulnerability, and we ask:

- Is it possible to go through the Valley of Weeping without falling apart?
- Is it possible to have joy in the midst of suffering?
- Is it possible to grow in intimacy with the Lord as we travel through the valley?

God and the psalmists say, "Yes," and I say, "Yes."

God has shown me that in my pain He wants to give me a blessing. With the psalmists,

> *I remember*
> > *I hide*
> > > *I cling*
> > > > *I journey*
> > > > > *AND*
> > > > *my Valley of Weeping becomes*
> > > > > *a Place of Blessing.*

With each page you turn, may God speak to your pain and reveal the blessing He has for you. May He take you to a deeper kind of calm.

THE SONG OF HOLY REMEMBERANCE

I cried out to God for help;
I cried out to God to hear me.
When I was in distress, I sought the
Lord;
at night I stretched out untiring
hands
and my soul refused to be
comforted.
I remembered you, O God, and I
groaned;
I mused, and my spirit grew faint.
You kept my eyes from closing;
I was too troubled to speak.
I thought about the former days,
the years of long ago;
I remembered my songs in the
night.
My heart mused and my spirit
inquired:
"Will the Lord reject forever?
Will he never show his favor again?
Has his unfailing love vanished
forever?
Has his promise failed for all time?

Has God forgotten to be merciful?
Has he in anger withheld his
compassion?"
Then I thought, "To this I will
appeal:
the years of the right hand of the
Most High."
I will remember the deeds of the
LORD;
yes, I will remember your miracles
of long ago.
I will meditate on all your works
and consider all your mighty deeds.
Your ways, O God, are holy.
What god is so great as our God?
You are the God who performs
miracles;
you display your power among the
peoples.
With your mighty arm you
redeemed your people,
the descendants of Jacob and
Joseph.
The waters saw you, O God,

the waters saw you and writhed;
the very depths were convulsed.
The clouds poured down water,
the skies resounded with thunder;
your arrows flashed back and forth.
Your thunder was heard in the
    whirlwind,
your lightning lit up the world;
the earth trembled and quaked.
Your path led through the sea,
your way through the mighty
    waters,
though your footprints were not
    seen.
You led your people like a flock
by the hand of Moses and Aaron.

PSALM 77

Chapter Two

I Remember

As I opened the door to my room, my heart began beating double-time. Something with razor-sharp teeth had gnawed the sealed water cup I'd left on the dresser—and more than likely, the varmint was still in my room!

Looking at the teeth marks on the cup, I shivered. *Not a rat! God, You know I hate rats.* I was staying at a retreat center outside of Kiev, Ukraine, where I was to speak to a group of missionary women. I knew it was God's plan that I was in Ukraine . . . but was a rat part of His plan? The thought of a loathsome, vile rodent sneaking around my room made my skin crawl. How could I sleep knowing that at any moment it might pounce on me or nibble my ear! Colorado bears I could tolerate, but Ukrainian rats pushed the limit.

Pacing up and down the room, I prayed: "God, I know You can give me sleep tonight regardless of the creepy thing crawling around this room. . . . I trust You. . . ." As these words escaped my lips, *swoosh!* Something near me moved. I screamed. (So much for trusting God!) Turning to face my intruder, I caught my breath. But instead of a rat, I saw a beautiful bird fluttering around my room.

Windows in Ukraine have no screens, and "Tweetie" had flown in my open window and pecked through the seal on my water cup with his beak. This lovely, yellow-breasted creature was "my rat." As Tweetie flew around my room, he left his "signature" on my suitcase, the dresser, and various other places. But a bird was not a rat, and I rejoiced.

The next morning Tweetie brought a friend to visit. The third morning he brought two friends. They circled around my room, landing on their favorite perch, the shower curtain pole. Each day as I spoke, I gave a "bird report." One hundred and fifty missionaries were staying at the retreat center, but only my room was blessed with Tweetie and friends.

As I packed my bags to travel to a different city to speak to Ukrainian leaders, I bid Tweetie farewell and thanked God for giving me a bird instead of a rat.

But life doesn't always work that way, does it? Sometimes we get rats instead of birds. Sometimes we need to trust God and rely on Him to help us deal with the things we hate.

This was certainly true for Natasha, a lovely young Ukrainian woman I met on that trip. She told me something I shall never forget.

Natasha occupied a wheelchair in the rear of the audience. Her handsome husband Sergei — the only man in the room — sat beside her to assist her. Later as I talked with Natasha and Sergei, I learned that fifteen months earlier she had been in a car accident that had left her paralyzed from the chest down. Paralyzed at twenty-five.

Natasha's words echoed in my ears: "Linda, I thought because I had committed my life to serve Christ that I would be blessed." Such thinking sounds like a reliable Christian formula.

> *Natasha says to God, "Yes, Lord, I'll walk Your path."*
> *God replies, "Good, Natasha, I'll bless you with health*
> *and happiness."*

What doesn't make sense is:

> *Natasha says to God, "Yes, Lord, I'll walk Your path."*
> *God replies, "Good, Natasha, I'll bless you with pain*
> *and suffering."*

In essence, Natasha got a rat instead of a bird. Rather than soaring toward her youthful dreams, she faced a life of confinement in a body that wouldn't move.

As I've traveled throughout the world and interacted with women from different cultures, one impression haunts me. No matter where I go, I see portraits of pain. Pain over a marriage gone sour, pain over a child gone astray, physical pain, emotional pain, spiritual pain. Pain is the persistent plague of our times. It creeps into our lives, stripping us of the joy and peace we claim is our portion as Christians.

Some of the most poignant passages ever penned about pain are recorded in the pages of the Old Testament. In the next few chapters, I want to take you on a journey into the lives of several psalmists who wrote about pain: David, Asaph, and the Sons of Korah. Each lived out an earthly story that endured much pain, and yet each in his own way learned how to see with the eyes of faith. Learning to see from God's perspective is critical if we are to turn our Valley of Weeping into a Place of Blessing, our sorrow into significance, our failures into faith.

Look with me at four choices that helped the psalmists do this:

- Psalm 77 — *I remember*
- Psalm 46 — *I hide*
- Psalm 63 — *I cling*
- Psalm 84 — *I journey*

Let's begin by diving into Psalm 77.

A HEART OF GRIEF

Have you ever been in such searing pain that you felt as if you were entombed in a deep, dark hole? Asaph, the author of Psalm 77 and one of King David's chief musicians, understood the depths of this piercing pain. Pain permeates his words and, although Asaph didn't identify the nature of his problem, he told God the depth of his agony and confusion. I'm sure a cascade of tears smudged the ink as he wrote.

> *I cried out to God for help; I cried out to God to hear me. When I was in distress, I sought the Lord; at night I stretched out untiring hands and my soul refused to be comforted. (verses 1-2)*

I love this man's honesty. He didn't mince words. With raw emotion, he revealed the doubt harbored in his soul. Even thinking about God made him groan. Yet in his desperate call for help, it is to God that he cried unceasingly. Asaph took his anguish to the only One who *could* intervene. This grief-stricken man lifted his hands all night in prayer to God, but God seemed removed and unconcerned. God had hidden His face. Although in agony of spirit, Asaph persisted.

The psalm continues:

> *I remembered you, O God, and I groaned; I mused, and my spirit grew faint. You kept my eyes from closing; I was too troubled to speak. (verses 3-4)*

Great grief has no words. Asaph cried out in his soul to God, but he could not speak to man. Sleepless and speechless, he watched through the night. Charles Spurgeon, a man of God and the author of *The Treasury of David*, knew this place of despair: "To spend nights in physical and spiritual anguish . . . I know this depressive state. My soul is familiar with this way of grief."[1]

I also am well acquainted with sleepless nights, dark nights when pain was so present and God seemed so distant that I couldn't open my Bible. It was full of promises of hope . . . but those promises didn't seem to apply to me, or to my children. This must have been how Asaph felt, because he began to pour out his doubts to God. In essence, he said, "Where are You, God? Where is Your mercy? Where are Your answers? Why are You silent when I need You? God, this pain is bad enough but without Your presence . . . without Your help . . . it is beyond measure."

Have you ever prayed something similar? I know I have. Just last week while studying Psalm 77 and Asaph's descent into despair, I received a phone call that broke my heart and sent me spiraling down to this dark place. One phone call opened an old wound, and once again my heart ached. I felt that I was living the pain-soaked statements found in the first eight verses of Psalm 77.

> *I search for God.*
> *I plead with Him.*
> *I can't sleep.*

I question God.

I compare.

I ask, "How long?"

I ask, "Where are God's promises?"

I am sure you also have known this place of pain. But the beautiful message of this psalm is that Asaph didn't *stay* in anguish! And he shares with us how he moved from the place of despair to a place of peace. Don't we need to understand how to do this? Natasha needed to know this as she sat in her wheelchair. After my devastating phone call, I needed to know how to move from despair to peace. And your heart needs to know this as well.

A HEART REMEMBERS

Something very dramatic happened in Asaph's heart in the second half of Psalm 77! *His sob of sorrow turned into a song of praise.*

What brought about this miraculous change? Three words express what he did:

I will remember.

This desperate man said:

- I will remember the deeds of the Lord. (verse 11)
- I will remember your miracles of long ago. (verse 11)

In Hebrew the word *remember* means "to call to mind again." This "calling to mind" isn't something that happens naturally. Asaph made a choice. The train of his mind was racing down a certain track—a track that led to despair—but suddenly he saw ahead a second track that veered off in a different direction, toward peace. In that moment he had to make a decision. Would he continue on his present course or would he "flip a switch" and travel in a new direction? He had to choose—quickly. He flipped the switch by saying three words: "I will remember." The train of his mind lurched, shifted, and moved onto the new track, taking his heart along with it.

Asaph made another choice that moved him even deeper into peace. This, too, is an "I will" statement:

> *I will meditate on all your works and consider all your mighty deeds. (verse 12)*

Notice that Asaph's words were not *I feel* but *I will*. *I will* indicates resolve. His choices to remember and to meditate on what God had done were *intentional* choices. And those choices transformed his pity party into a praise celebration. As his focus shifted from his problem to God's promises, he reasoned, "If God has been so faithful in the past, surely He will be faithful in the present . . . and in the future."

In essence he said, "Today all is dark. I can't see what God is doing, but instead of staying here and letting the problem paralyze me, I *will* turn my mind to what God has done in the past. Today I see no miracles, so I *will* turn my mind to the miracles in Israel's history. And I won't just acknowledge them, I *will* meditate on what God has done. I *will* go over and over and over *all* the works and mighty deeds of the Lord. I *will* recall God's faithfulness to Moses and relive the crossing of the Red Sea."

We see Asaph's change in perspective in the way he wrote the psalm. In the first part of the psalm, Asaph used *I, me,* and *my* twenty-two times. Eleven times he referred to God by name, title, or pronoun. But *after* he remembered, he referred to God twenty-four times and referred to himself only three times—in the three *I wills!* Asaph lifted his eyes off of his desperate situation, where all he could see was himself, to his great God, who is majestic, mighty, and a worker of miracles.

This was Asaph's part: *I will remember.* "I will make a conscious choice not to travel on the track of pain that descends into darkness; instead, I will shift to the track that embraces *who* God is and *what* He has done in the past."

When pain-filled circumstances fill our focus, we are like blind people. All is dark. But remembering lifts the scales off our spiritual eyes. Remembering brings God's promises to the forefront of our minds. God promises that *all* things (including this dark time you are in now) will work together for good (see Romans 8:28). Yes, God says He will work character, perseverance, and hope in your life through this hard time (see Romans 5:3-5).

Perhaps you know these blessed truths but, like me, you forget them in the midst of the Valley of Weeping. Your eyes can't see beyond the fog of despair. Turn your eyes! *Remember; remember and meditate!*

MY HEART REMEMBERS

Asaph — this dear, honest man — has been my teacher since 1984 when he inspired me to write my first "I remember" list. Forcing myself from my warm bed, I wrote my list of God's mighty works and deeds during the past year in the life of the teenager who had burdened my heart. As I saw in black and white how God had been at work, my heart could trust Him for what I could not see that day. This list was lost in a move from Austria to Hong Kong, but my "I remembers" went something like this:

1. I've seen a glimpse of spiritual interest.
2. I recall three deep talks with my child.
3. I see how You have protected my child.
4. I remember the positive friend You brought into my child's life.
5. I can see how Jody's and my relationship with this child has improved.

As I wrote my "remembrances," a strange thing happened. I began to think about what God had done in my life through the anguish over my child. The list changed as I continued.

6. I am learning to trust You on a deeper level.

7. I am learning to give up control.

8. I am experiencing more peace in the midst of the circumstance I don't like.

God often uses someone else's trouble to work in our own lives. May I give you some examples? Madam Guyon's sweetest poems and deepest experiences came in the midst of long imprisonments. She made this astute observation: "When one loves what God is doing in one's life, one cannot hate the instrument through which it comes." Paul wrote many of his epistles in prison cells; John wrote Revelation while in exile; John Bunyan penned *Pilgrim's Progress* in the Bedford jail; Martin Luther translated the German Bible as a prisoner in Warburg Castle.[2] Similarly, walking through seasons of pain has been the schoolroom where I have gone deeper in knowing the Holy One as the Blessed Controller of All Things. Intimacy with my Bridegroom has blossomed in the prison of pain.

Since 1984 I've written more "I remember" lists than I can count. As with Asaph, remembering has spurred my heart to trust and see God as holy. And so I have encouraged others to do the same.

Natasha's "I Remember" List

Natasha sat in her wheelchair. I sat in front of her, my hands holding hers. Through a translator we talked and prayed for two hours. Looking into her eyes, I helped her begin her "I remember" list. "Natasha, I want to tell you what I see:

1. I see a husband and wife who look at one another with piercing love in their eyes.
2. I see a husband and wife who speak secrets to one another with their glances.
3. I see an intimacy that few couples ever experience.

"Tell me, Natasha. What has God done in the past year in the midst of this terrible trial?"

Together Natasha, Sergei, and I completed the list:

4. Their son was protected during the accident. (Natasha shielded him with her body.)
5. Although Natasha was in the hospital for a year, their son is a happy, healthy four-year-old.
6. Natasha has a new vision of how God can use her pain to minister to women.

And wonder of wonders:

7. Natasha's parents are interested in the Lord and coming to church.

For eleven years since becoming a Christian, Natasha had begged God to touch her parents' hearts and draw them to Christ, yet they had remained very opposed to her faith. In the times of "plenty" they could not see the benefits of Jesus. But through the year of darkness, pain had softened their hearts in a way that pleasure never could. I told Natasha that I believed her whole family would come to Christ.

When I asked Natasha if she had heard of Joni Eareckson Tada, she said yes, she had read Joni's books in Russian. I smiled and said, "Perhaps God is preparing you to be the Joni Eareckson of Ukraine." God is writing Natasha and Sergei's story in the heavens. They can't see all His purposes; life is difficult and will continue to be very difficult, but "remembering" lifted their eyes from the earthly, daily drudgery of wheelchairs to God's higher purpose.

I made my remember list. Natasha made hers. My friend, will you take pen and paper, find a quiet place to be alone with your God, and make your list? When we remember, our spiritual eyes are opened, and we see the truth about God that our physical eyes have missed.

A Heart That Sees

As Asaph remembered, the fog was lifted from his spiritual eyes and he saw that God's ways, even though beyond understanding, were right and holy.

> *Your ways, O God, are holy. What God is so great as our God? You are the God who performs miracles;*

> *you display your power among the peoples. With your*
> *mighty arm you redeemed your people. (verses 13-15)*

Every one of us walks through Valleys of Weeping—some deep, some not so deep. Family and friends can encourage and comfort us as we walk along the path of pain, but ultimately each of us must make the choice to turn our hearts to remember. Only you can turn your mind to think on God's works and wonders and allow the God who remembers all to flood your soul with His past goodness—in world history and in your "personal history." As you dwell on His goodness, the eyes of your heart will see that He will again be good.

Oh, how often we are commanded in Scripture to remember what God has done. Over and over God pleads, "Do not forget."

> *Give heed to yourself and keep your soul diligently, lest*
> *you forget the things which your eyes have seen, and lest*
> *they depart from your heart. (Deuteronomy 4:9, NASB)*

> *And you shall remember all the way which the LORD*
> *your God has led you in the wilderness. (Deuteronomy*
> *8:2, NASB)*

The Israelites were great "forgetters," but so are we. God wants us to be remembering people. We must covenant with God to remember. Will you, like Asaph, tell Him you long to be one who remembers?

I will remember the deeds of the LORD; yes, I will
remember your miracles of long ago. I will meditate
on all your works and consider all your mighty deeds.
(verses 11-12)

Will you remember all God's works and mighty deeds to you
personally?

When you remember, you can yield to God and say:

> *Even though Your ways*
> *Are not my ways,*
> *Even though Your timing is not my timing,*
> *Even though I see no end to this pain,*
> > *I trust You.*

> *And*
> *I remember*
> *Your ways in the past,*
> *Your timing in the past;*
> *So even though I can't see*
> *Today or in the future,*
> *Remembering turns my pain into*
> *Praise.*
> *Praise because of who You are,*
> *Praise because of what You*
> *Have done in the past.*
> *Praise because of what You*
> *Will do now.*

As the following illustration so beautifully shows, sometimes as we remember and open the eyes of faith, God reveals His purposes:

> *My mother's father worked as a carpenter. On this particular day, he was building some crates for the clothes his church was sending to orphanages in China. On his way home, he reached into his shirt pocket to find his glasses, but they were gone. When he mentally replayed his earlier actions, he realized what had happened; the glasses had slipped out of his pocket unnoticed and fallen into one of the crates, which he had nailed shut. His brand-new glasses were headed for China!*
>
> *The Great Depression was at its height and Grandpa had six children. He had spent $20 for those glasses that very morning. He was upset by the thought of having to buy another pair. "It's not fair," he told God as he drove home in frustration. "I've been very faithful in giving of my time and money to Your work, and now this."*
>
> *Months later, the director of the orphanage was on furlough in the United States. He wanted to visit all the churches that supported him in China, so he came to speak one Sunday at my grandfather's small church in Chicago. The missionary began by thanking the people*

*for their faithfulness in supporting the orphanage. "But
most of all," he said, "I must thank you for the glasses
you sent last year. You see, the Communists had just
swept through the orphanage, destroying everything,
including my glasses. I was desperate. Even if I had had
the money, there was simply no way of replacing those
glasses. Along with not being able to see well, I experienced headaches every day, so my coworkers and I were
much in prayer about this. Then your crates arrived.
When my staff removed the covers, they found a pair of
glasses lying on top." The missionary paused long enough
to let his words sink in. Then, still gripped with the
wonder of it all, he continued: "Folks, when I tried on
the glasses, it was as if they had been custom made just
for me. I want to thank you for being a part of that."*

*The people listened, happy for the miraculous
glasses. But the missionary surely must have confused
their church with another, they thought. There were
no glasses on their list of items to be sent overseas. But
sitting quietly in the back, with tears streaming down
his face, an ordinary carpenter realized the Master
Carpenter had used him in an extraordinary way.*[3]

Sometimes God allows us to see why He lets the glasses fall
into crates bound for China; other times He doesn't. As far as we
know, Asaph never received clarification from God concerning

his deep pain. But when he turned his heart to remember *who* God was and *what* God had done in the past, his eyes were lifted above his earthly story of loss and pain and God began to give him a deeper kind of calm.

God lifted Natasha's eyes above her earthly circumstances, and He continually lifts my perspective. I've been on the path of remembering for nineteen years, and it has made an incredible difference in my life. My friend, will you choose to walk this path? Even when God does not reveal the why of your pain, He will lift your spiritual eyes and fill your heart with joy . . . when you say,

I will remember.

THE SONG OF HOLY CONFIDENCE

God is our refuge and strength,
an ever-present help in trouble.
Therefore we will not fear, though
*   the earth give way*
and the mountains fall into the
*   heart of the sea,*
though its waters roar and foam
and the mountains quake with
*   their surging.*
There is a river whose streams
*   make glad the city of God,*
the holy place where the Most High
*   dwells.*
God is within her, she will not fall;
God will help her at break of day.
Nations are in uproar, kingdoms
*   fall;*
he lifts his voice, the earth melts.
The LORD Almighty is with us;
the God of Jacob is our fortress.
Come and see the works of the
*   LORD,*
the desolations he has brought on
*   the earth.*

He makes wars cease to the ends of
*   the earth;*
he breaks the bow and shatters the
*   spear,*
he burns the shields with fire.
"Be still, and know that I am God;
I will be exalted among the nations,
I will be exalted in the earth."
The LORD Almighty is with us;
the God of Jacob is our fortress.

PSALM 46

Chapter Three

I Hide

My feet stumbled along the uneven path. Barney, the most sensitive dog God ever created, knew where we were going. He heard my sobs before they escaped my lips. Scrambling over the sandstone boulders, I lifted my eyes. There it was — my hiding place, my refuge carved by the Almighty. Behind my home at the front range of the Rocky Mountains is a rock park. It is my personal sanctuary. As Barney and I squeezed through the narrow opening in the rock, my heart calmed. High walls engulfed me — I was safe, hidden in the cleft of the rock.

Tears streamed down my face as I leaned against my strong shelter. As my eyes scaled the fifteen-foot height of the rock enclosure, I prayed through Psalm 46 as I poured out my heart to God.

> *God, I can't go on. These daily migraines have beaten me down. I feel like giving up. I have run here to my rock refuge to remind myself that You alone are my refuge. You alone are my strength. Right now I choose to run into You . . . into the shelter of Your arms. Truly You alone are my fortress. My personal "earth" is crashing down around me. . . . I feel like the mountains have fallen into the sea. . . . Thank you that You say I do not need to fear. O God, You are the Blessed Controller of All Things, including my migraines. You alone will be exalted over all the earth. . . . Please be exalted over my little "earth." I know I must be still to experience the safety and security of You as my rock of refuge. Teach me, Holy One, to be still and know that You are God.*

I had run into my rock refuge ready to give up on life, defeated by the pounding pain above my right eye. When I walked away from my sanctuary, my head was still hammering, but God had infused me with strength and a determination to keep going. My despair had changed to hope, and spiritually I felt enveloped by the refuge of His presence.

In the last chapter you learned from Psalm 77 how *remembering* what God has done could change your sob of doubt to a song of praise. From Psalm 46 you will learn how you can *hide* in God.

Come with me, and let's look together at the glorious promises in this magnificent forty-sixth psalm known as Martin Luther's Psalm. I pray that you will be encouraged to hide in your refuge . . . that fear will be cast away because the Lord Almighty is *your* personal refuge, *your* personal strength and fortress! No trial that has wrapped itself around your life is too difficult for Him.

MARTIN LUTHER'S FAVORITE PSALM

The Song of Holy Confidence, Psalm 46, carries an important message for our hearts: *No matter what storm sweeps across our lives, we can hide in the secure refuge of His presence.* Throughout the centuries, many (including me) have loved this strong word of encouragement. Martin Luther's name is often associated with the book of Romans and justification by faith, but Luther also loved the Psalms and taught them for many years. During the difficult and dark days of the Reformation, when Luther became discouraged, he would turn to his colleague Philipp Melanchthon and say, "My friend, let's go sing the forty-sixth!" The promises of this psalm so lifted Luther's spirit that he wrote a majestic hymn around its message, "A Mighty Fortress Is Our God."

When discouraged and sinking into depression, Luther hid in the One who was "high and lifted up," and there he felt secure. This man of God needed a refuge because of the many attacks against him after he nailed his Ninety-Five Theses to the church door at Wittenberg. I needed a refuge because blinding migraine headaches had kept me in survival mode for months. And, my friend, you need a place to hide when life overwhelms you. And Scripture promises that God Almighty will be your refuge and fortress! When your personal world seems out of control, the glorious promises of Psalm 46 are just what you need.

- God is your refuge. (verse 1)
- God is your help. (verse 1)
- God is your fortress. (verse 7)

God Is Your Refuge

Tonight as I was reflecting on my life and the times I have needed a refuge, two very different situations came to mind. The first was when I was caught in a typhoon in Hong Kong. Winds swirled, rain pounded, and I couldn't see two feet in front of me. Tears mixed with the pelting rain as I blindly stumbled around seeking refuge. When I finally found the shelter of a tall building, my relief was overpowering. I leaned against the wall and released huge gulping sobs. The second time I needed a refuge was in 1985 when security police in Communist Romania were hunting for Jody and me. A Romanian friend went quickly to our hotel and gathered our belongings, then hid us in a car and drove to the Hungarian border. During the long ride, I was sure Jody could hear my racing heartbeat. Only when we were secure in a Budapest hotel did my heart quiet. Both times, a building provided refuge.

The *Oxford Dictionary* defines *refuge* as a place of "shelter from pursuit or danger or trouble." But Psalm 46 assures me that *my* refuge is not a place but a Person. According to this psalm, Jehovah, the Mighty One, is also the Merciful One who bends down and listens to my cry for help. He is my refuge from the storms of life. He is my strength when enemies pursue me. One of my enemies is named Migraine. I run to God for refuge against this enemy. I also go to Him for strength to withstand the attacks of another enemy that follows in close pursuit behind Migraine. Its name is Discouragement.

Who or what enemy do you face today? Your enemy may be a person, but it also can be anxiety, depression, fear, or despair. When assaulted by enemies, we are tempted to run to something or someone other than God for comfort. But Psalm 46 emphatically declares that God *alone* is our refuge. He gives two kinds of help. He is a stronghold into which we can flee, and He is a source of inner strength by which we can face every trial. God is *my personal refuge, your personal refuge.* Our God is all-sufficient; His defense can surpass that of any and every enemy. And what does our personal refuge promise us? There is no time, situation, or trial for which He does not send His help.

God Is Your Help

God is described as "an ever-present help in trouble" (Psalm 46:1). How I love the word *ever-present*! My Rock of Refuge stands on guard to protect me, day and night, summer and winter, in sickness and in health, from discouragement and harm. My God never withdraws Himself from me when I am hurting, crushed, and ready to give up. He is my help; truly, constantly, always near me, and ready to give comfort. Closer than any friend or husband, mother, father, or child, He sends help right when I need it. This glorious truth reassures me when my "earth" gives way. It boosts my confidence when God "feels" far away, removed from my personal problems. Because God Almighty, all-powerful, all-loving, is *my personal refuge*, I don't need to fear—today, tomorrow, or ever.

As you read Psalm 46, notice how David uses two big "thoughs" to describe four catastrophic events. "Therefore we will not fear, *though* the earth give way and the mountains fall into the heart of the sea, *though* its waters roar and foam and the mountains quake with their surging" (verses 2-3, emphasis added). If the earth should break apart in such a gigantic, disastrous way that the Rocky Mountains fall into the Pacific Ocean . . . even then I don't need to fear. I am hidden in God my refuge, sheltered safely under His wings.

After the deaths of her first two husbands, Elisabeth Elliott felt this kind of catastrophic breaking apart of her life: "Everything that has seemed most dependable has given way. Mountains are falling, earth is reeling. In such a time it is a profound comfort to know that although all things seem to be shaken, one thing is not: God is not shaken."[1] Elisabeth Elliott knew as her help the

One whose name is the Lord Almighty.

My friend Mimi hid in the strong name of her God while living in Jordan. Her husband's boss had been assassinated days before, and fear permeated the city of Amman. Talk of evacuation and chemical warfare occurred daily. Mimi cried out to God with these words:

> *Cover me, my God. Cover me! The facts I know about You and Your character are not enough for my heart to find comfort if I do not let my soul sink into the strength of Your mighty name. Psalm 46:11 says, "The LORD Almighty is with us." I am asking You, God, to cover me with all of Your character so only what is filtered after going through all those layers will even touch me. The world may be drowning in the horror of evil, but I am wrapped safely in Your character. What comes through to me was designed by Your love to purify me and not to harm me. So I walk today surrounded by my personal Refuge. You are my Help in time of trouble. I am at peace.*

God Is Your Fortress

God is your refuge and help. He is also your fortress.

For many years I lived in Europe where fortresses are commonplace. Great impregnable structures adorn the Rhine and Danube rivers in Germany and Austria. Because we have not had a war on American soil for more than a century, our nation has become wrapped in a cocoon of false security. Pre-9/11 we didn't need fortresses — post-9/11 we search frantically for fortress-like protection against the elusive enemy of terrorism. Post-Columbine our high schools have taken on fortress-like status. As I write these words, my son and his family in Montgomery County, Maryland, are praying that their locked, darkened home will stand as a fortress against the sniper who has killed at will — whenever, wherever, whomever he chooses. All of Washington, D.C., has taken on a "fortress mentality."

When I think of fortresses, one in particular stands out — Masada. Perhaps you have read *Masada* or seen the movie of the same name. My heart aches when I think of the brave Israelites hidden high in the fortress of Masada, holding off Roman troops for almost two years. This mountain fort could only be entered by way of a steep trail known as Snake Pass because of snakes in the area and the snake-like way the trail wound up the mountain. Masada was secure — until the Roman legions discovered a way to topple the walled city on the hill.

In her book *The Hiding Place*, Corrie ten Boom describes how, during the Nazi terror, her family fled to their personal fortress in a hidden closet at the top of their house. Shaking, quietly sobbing, they waited in their refuge for the disaster to pass. Time and time again their "hiding place" proved a worthy fortress . . . until Nazi axes broke through the wall and they were taken to concentration camps.

Manmade fortresses always eventually fail. But there is a fortress — a high fortress, a secure fortress — that will never fail! This fortress is not a place, but a Person. His name is the Lord Almighty!

My friend, Donna, knows this to be true.

Donna's Fortress

While I was fighting migraines, Donna also struggled with unwelcome intruders. Seven illnesses had taken over her body; the interplay of two of them created such havoc that she was unable to breathe. Still, Donna kept her great sense of humor. For example, after seeing her struggle for breath one too many times, I drew a line in the sand and said, "From now on, you *always* take your oxygen with you." Donna immediately quipped that an oxygen tank just wasn't a proper accessory to *any* outfit.

Donna was an athlete until the thief called Illness stole her breath. But being a *very* determined woman, she continued to play team tennis. Finally another friend and I told her, "If you play tennis again, we're kneeling on the sides of the tennis court as you smash the ball over the net. Don't let us bother you . . . we'll just be praying that you come to your senses!" Because she feared we would do what we said, and her tennis partners feared she would collapse on the court, Donna gave up tennis. She gave up many things, and not one was easy.

I remember one summer day in particular when she was in the hospital in Denver. I had a migraine but took heavy medicine so I could be with her while the doctors tried yet another intravenous regimen to force her lungs to breathe. As I sat by my friend's bed, I thought, *I face pain but Donna faces death. And not just physical death, but the death of her dreams—of being at her son's wedding, of holding her future grandbabies, of growing old with her husband.* I asked Donna to tell me how she does it. How can she have such a childlike trust in God when she lives with daily pain? How does she deal with the fact that tomorrow may never come? Here is her reply:

> *God is my refuge and strength. These are simple words with an ocean's depth of truth. When my world falls apart and I do not know how I can get through the next hour, when my breathing is labored and the oxygen turned to max, I run to the only One who can bring me peace — I run to God. I feel His loving arms around me. He picks me up, sets me in His lap, and holds me close. I am safe. God renews my strength and keeps me keeping on until He calls me home.*
>
> *God is my refuge and my peace. How do I come into this refuge? I come through prayer with thanksgiving, thanking God because He is in control. I praise Him for His sovereignty and believe all His promises. I am in the eye of the storm, at peace and full of love for my Savior*

Jesus Christ.

As others watch me and ask why I am not afraid,
I tell them it is because I know the living God and He
is with me. In the midst of pain, I have joy. God is my
fortress, my security, my hope in all kinds of trouble.
When I cry out His name, I am there in my refuge — for
that minute, hour, day. He does not disappoint. Words
are just not enough to represent my Lord; I must do it
with my life, and with every breath I take.

Donna sees God as her strong, secure refuge, and also as her Father who tenderly cares for her. When we see our God this way—as the high and lifted up Holy One who set the stars in the heavens and created the whole earth—we will find Him to be our strong, secure fortress as well. The Holy One longs to be our refuge, our help, and our fortress. Amazing! Our Mighty God gets tenderly personal and intimately involved in our "little earthly life."

Let's look at three important choices you and I can make that will teach us how to hide in God as our refuge:

1. Be still before Him.
2. Have faith in Him.
3. Flee into Him.

Be Still Before Him

"Be still, and know that I am God; I will be exalted
among the nations, I will be exalted in the earth."
(Psalm 46:10)

Psalm 46 clearly says that in order to know that God controls all the fearful happenings of this world, you must be still. Is all confusion for you today? Is your world falling apart? God longs for you to know that even though you can't see how the problem will work out for good, He will be exalted in all the earth . . . and in your "personal earth." How can you be assured of this? You will never know . . . unless you can be still. When my enemy, Migraine, throws darts at me, I must quiet my fears, kneel with patience in God's presence, and listen. Then and only then will I be assured that He is God.

But I have difficulty sitting down and being quiet. When a problem erupts in my life, I want to take action! I want to DO something—anything—but be still. An entry in my journal verifies this:

O God, shut off the frantic noisiness of my words. Teach
me how to be with You in silence — to listen and not
speak. James' admonition to be swift to hear and slow
to speak applies in my relationship with You as well as
with people. Let me learn as Elijah learned that You are

in the quiet whisper, not the earth-shattering thunder.
How often have I missed You because of my excessive
clamor?
Do I know what it means to "be still and know that
[You are] God"? To cease striving? Does anyone know?
God, I want to discover silence. Silence with only You,
with the flow of my words turned off and my heart
turned to worship and wait, bowed before My Father.

God gave me a picture of how I might be still in Him one night as I tried to quiet my noisy newborn granddaughter, Annika. I wrapped her tiny body tightly in her blanket, held her securely against my warmth, then rocked and sang to her until her frantic cries ceased. In my arms she felt secure enough to sleep—you guessed it—like a baby! My prayer at that moment was, *God, help me learn to let Your presence quiet me. Teach me how to throw myself totally on You. Hold me against Your warmth and quiet my soul with Your singing.*

Silence and solitude are becoming my friends. In them I find His presence and know that He is God.

HAVE FAITH IN HIM

Psalm 18:2 says that God is "my rock, in whom I take refuge." The Hebrew word for *refuge* in this verse, *hasah,* means "to trust." So, to take refuge in God is to trust Him.[2] Faith hopes in *who* God is and in *what* He has promised. Trust in what God says, not in what you see. "Who . . . walks in darkness and has no light? Let him trust in the name of the LORD and rely on his God" (Isaiah 50:10, NASB). Donna chooses to trust God each day. So must you and I. We must consciously choose to trust and rely upon God. This means we give up relying on our clever ways of massaging the circumstances, of manipulating people (this includes husbands and children), or of maneuvering around God's will. It means humbly bowing and saying to God,

> *I trust You.*
> *I trust Your ways.*
> *I trust Your timing.*
> *I hide in You.*

Oh, the peace of yielding to His ways, His timing, and His will! When we truly bow before Him as the Blessed Controller of *All* Things, the small problems that slowly tear us apart and the gigantic ones that crash over us like a tsunami wave do not uproot us. We are nestled in the Holy One, our refuge . . . safe and sheltered in the haven of His wings.

Flee into Him

My friend, I long to direct your heart into this place of refuge! Are winds swirling about you? Run into the Lord! A refuge is something you *flee into*. A refuge doesn't automatically erect itself around you; you have to seek it out and run into its shelter for safe harbor. As God's Word says, "We who have *fled to him for refuge* can take new courage, for we can hold on to his promise with confidence. This confidence is like a strong and trustworthy anchor for our souls" (Hebrews 6:18-19, NLT, emphasis added). If you want God to be your refuge, flee into Him. Cry, "O Lord, I am about to be consumed—I run into You! Hide me!"[3]

Run to your refuge. Visualize yourself hiding in His protective care. Look at how King David did this:

- David visualized himself in the refuge of a rock: "For in the day of trouble he will keep me safe in his dwelling; he will hide me in the shelter of his tabernacle and set me high upon a rock." (Psalm 27:5)
- David imagined that God was enveloping him as a shield: "But you are a shield around me, O LORD." (Psalm 3:3)

When Martin Luther needed to flee into the refuge of the Lord, he sang the hymn he wrote from Psalm 46: "A mighty fortress is our God, a bulwark never failing." When I need to run to God, I picture myself in the cleft of rock behind my house. As I do, my mind lifts to my spiritual rock of refuge. Perhaps it would help you hide in God if you listened to a recording of a choir singing "A Mighty Fortress Is Our God" and then pictured yourself nestled in a fortress high on a hill, or if you fell to your knees, closed your eyes, and saw God placing His protective care not just before you as a shield but completely around you. God desires that we use our minds to direct our hearts to the safety of the hiding place of His refuge.

I remember when my son was small and terror struck his heart during a severe thunderstorm. As the thunder cracked, he raced as fast as his little legs could move and threw himself into my arms. "Mommy, Mommy, hold me. Hold me tight!" Lifting Tommy onto my lap, I enfolded him in my strong, secure grasp, and his cries eventually ceased. Sighs replaced sobs, and peace reigned.

Do you see? Do you understand? Your Father God waits for you . . . longs for you to run and leap into His arms. He will lift you, His precious child, onto His lap and encircle you in the shelter of His presence. As you flee into His refuge, as His strength seeps into you, a glorious peace will reign in your heart. *God will be your personal Rock of Refuge.*

When smoke and ash from the Hayman fire swirled toward our home, Barney and I again walked out to my cleft in the rock. As I prayed, I looked at the pine trees that I loved and thought of my wonderful home built of wood, and I lifted it all to Him as a sacrifice. "Lord, I've told you before that it is all Yours. And I'm saying it again . . . all belongs to You." As I imagined what my sanctuary would look like sans trees, shrubs, wildflowers, and every living thing, I thought, *The only thing that would remain would be my rock of refuge. The fiercest storm cannot topple it. Fire cannot destroy it. My refuge would still be here amidst the blackened world.*

My friend, no matter how much ash and smoke cloud your vision today, no matter if the mountains of your life are falling into the sea, your Rock of Refuge *will* always be there. Run into Him. Hide in Him.

> *My God, I want to know You as my refuge in the midst of this problem. I long to experience that You alone are my strength and my help. O God, You are my fortress. Teach me to be still so I can learn. I run into You. Hide me!*
>
> *O my God, "Be my rock of refuge, to which I can always go." (Psalm 71:3)*

The Song of Holy Longing

O God, you are my God,
earnestly I seek you;
my soul thirsts for you,
my body longs for you,
in a dry and weary land
where there is no water.
I have seen you in the sanctuary
and beheld your power and your
  glory.
Because your love is better than
  life,
my lips will glorify you.
I will praise you as long as I live,
and in your name I will lift up my
  hands.
My soul will be satisfied as with
  the richest of foods;
with singing lips my mouth will
  praise you.
On my bed I remember you;
I think of you through the watches
  of the night.
Because you are my help,
I sing in the shadow of your wings.

My soul clings to you;
your right hand upholds me.
They who seek my life will be
  destroyed;
they will go down to the depths of
  the earth.
They will be given over to the
  sword
and become food for jackals.
But the king will rejoice in God;
all who swear by God's name will
  praise him,
while the mouths of liars will be
  silenced.

PSALM 63

Chapter Four

I Cling

Though it happened many years ago, the memory remains vivid in my mind. It was the day I learned that heights and I do not do well together. My high school P.E. teacher had insisted that everyone in the class climb a pole to the top of the gym. Hand over hand, I shimmied up the pole, thinking, *This isn't so hard.* But then I made the mistake of looking down, and I panicked. My eyes glassed over, my hands let go, and I started sliding down . . . down . . . down. Screams from the gym floor jolted me and I grabbed the pole and pasted my shaking body around it. I held on to the cold steel with a death grip. No way was I coming down. I was clinging—sticking like glue—to the pole.

I don't remember how I finally got down, but I know I told the teacher that even if it meant getting an F, I would never go up that pole again.

Little did I know that my pole-clinging experience was biblical—but it was! God wants us to cling to Him the way I clutched that pole—as if our life depends on it! The Hebrew word *dabaq*, translated in Psalm 63 as cling, literally means "to stick like glue."

Women have experience with stick-like-glue clinging. Every young mother knows the clinging of a small child. I remember when I had three toddlers wrapped around my knees like Saran Wrap. How I longed for a little "unstuck" time! And what woman hasn't looked in the mirror after dressing, only to see the fabric hugging the fat deposits she wants so desperately to hide. Last week as I was trying on a dress at a department store, the view of my posterior molded by the clingy fabric made me gasp in horror. Never had a dress come off so fast!

I think you have captured the vision of stick-like-glue clinging. In this chapter the psalmist David will take us beyond gym poles, cellulite-hugging fabrics, and clingy toddlers to teach us what it means to cling to the Almighty One. To comprehend David's message on clinging, we need to look at another aspect of *dabaq* that suggests the idea of clinging to a person with the purpose of demonstrating loyalty and affection. This Hebrew word is translated interchangeably as *cling* or *cleave*.

LOYALTY AND AFFECTION

We see the concept of clinging beautifully portrayed in the marriage relationship. "For this cause a man shall leave his father and mother, and shall cleave [cling] to his wife; and the two shall become one flesh" (Ephesians 5:31, NASB). The holy, intoxicating one-flesh intimacy in marriage happens when a husband and wife "stick like glue" to one another.

We experience delight when we cling to our marriage partner with affection and loyalty. And we delight God when we cling to Him with love and affection. Moses understood this, and he commanded the Israelites to cling to their God:

> *You shall fear the LORD your God; you shall serve Him and cling to Him, and you shall swear by His name. He is your praise and He is your God, who has done these great and awesome things for you which your eyes have seen. (Deuteronomy 10:20-21, NASB)*

In Joshua's farewell message to the Israelites, he pleaded with them *not* to cling to the ways of the idolatrous foreign cultures but instead to cling to the Lord:

> *Only be very careful to observe the commandment and the law which Moses the servant of the LORD commanded you, to love the LORD your God and walk in all His ways and keep His commandments and hold*

*fast [cling] to Him and serve Him with all your heart
and with all your soul. (Joshua 22:5, NASB)*

King David was a man who knew about clinging to His God.
Psalm 63 demonstrates how he clung to God in his Valley of
Weeping and the difference it made in his life.

THE PSALM OF HOLY CLINGING

Psalm 63 is unquestionably one of the most beautiful and touch-
ing of the psalms. Throughout the centuries, the early fathers of
the church decreed and ordained that no day should pass without
the public singing of this psalm written by the former shepherd
boy who was king over Israel.[1]

What comes to your mind when you think of David? He was:

- A man after God's own heart.
- A man forgiven much.
- A man who walked intimately with God.
- A man who praised seven times a day.

But though David is known for his great triumphs and his close
relationship with God, he was a man well acquainted with grief.
Often he walked through the Valley of Weeping. His feet trod
that path when King Saul, his beloved mentor, turned on him
and tried to kill him. Oh, the pain of a friend—a mentor—
hunting you down, scouring the earth to find you and take your

life. David wrote many psalms while hiding in caves from Saul. But the sting of Saul's betrayal pales compared to the anguish David felt as he wrote Psalm 63.

Absalom — the son David had bounced on his knee, held to his breast, and carried on his shoulders; the son he had taught to run, ride, and shoot an arrow straight to the mark — now ran swiftly after David with an arrow pointed at his father's heart.

Anyone who has given life, love, and blessing to a child and received in return rejection, defection, and desolation understands a little of what David felt. Maggie knew David's distress:

> *My goal as a mother was to love and train my son to be a disciple of Christ. As a Christian leader, nothing would thrill my heart more than to see my son become a servant of God. Was I a perfect mother? Far from it, but I loved my son and gave all I knew how to give — of my heart, my time, my creativity . . . my all.*
>
> *My son is twenty-two. He is a "disciple" — not of the Creator God but of the god of pleasure. He lives for whatever his body and emotions desire. Sexual pleasure and drugs are his food. He laughs at my "archaic" ideas about God. My daily portion is a broken heart.*

Can you begin to imagine the terrible pain Maggie carries daily? Can you imagine the agony David bore as he hid in the wilderness fleeing from his own son? What thoughts poured from David's pen as he walked through the valley of grief? You might expect him to curse God. Amazingly, we read NOT of cursing, but of blessing, and of a passionate thirst for God. In the midst of pain and pressure, David penned this Psalm of Holy Longing for God. Through his beautiful poetic words, he shows us how to cling.

Four attitudes caused David's heart to cling:

1. He longed for God.
2. He found satisfaction in God.
3. He had an intimate friendship with God.
4. He had a desperate dependence on God.

Let's take an in-depth look at each of these. As we do, ask God to show you in a deeper way what it means for you to cling to Him.

David Longed for God

> O God, you are my God, earnestly I seek you; my soul
> thirsts for you, my body longs for you, in a dry and
> weary land where there is no water. I have seen you in
> the sanctuary and beheld your power and your glory.
> (verses 1-2)

David craved God! The godly preacher Charles Spurgeon said that such holy desires stir our inner nature more than any other influence. Only God can satisfy the craving of a soul aroused by the Holy Spirit.[2]

I am well acquainted with cravings. In three months I celebrate my sixtieth birthday, and my goal is to lose twenty pounds and firm up the flab before that milepost occasion. I'm in my second month of food deprivation, and I could make you a *long* list of my cravings. Yes, my taste buds covet chocolate, popcorn, and homemade bread, but as I read about David's longing for God, I ask myself, "Do I crave God? Are my taste buds starved for Him?"

David did not hunger for food (or chocolate) but only for God. He had seen God's glory. He knew God's power. He pursued God with his whole heart, and in that pursuit, God met him and satisfied the longings of his soul.

David Found Satisfaction in God

Because your love is better than life, my lips will glorify you. I will praise you as long as I live, and in your name I will lift up my hands. My soul will be satisfied as with the richest of foods; with singing lips my mouth will praise you. (verses 3-5)

God's presence was David's daily bread. Only God's love could satisfy him. Do we even have a glimmer of understanding of God's love? Can we say with David that God's love is better than life?

Most of us love life more than we love God. We hang on to life because we value it more than anything else we possess. We will gladly give our money and credit cards to a thief rather than be shot. We will endure painful surgeries in the hope that our days on this earth will be multiplied. But David says there is something more precious than life—the love of God! David experienced firsthand the *hesed*, or loving kindness, of God—a covenant love that is ever steady and unchangeable. As David dwelt on this love, praise erupted from his lips.

David praised God verbally and physically. He praised the Most High God with words, song, and hands raised high. I can almost hear his exuberant shouts and joyful hallelujahs. David was excited about God! God's love so overwhelmed him that he had to worship the Holy One with body, soul, and spirit.

David Had an Intimate Friendship with God

> *On my bed I remember you; I think of you through the watches of the night. Because you have been my help, I sing in the shadow of your wings. (verses 6-7)*

David had a secret life with God, a life of intimate friendship that no one saw. Though his whole being agonized over the breach with his son, his heart rejoiced in the night as he clung to his God. David's intimate connection to God enabled him to cast his problem on God and feel such peace that songs flowed from his lips!

I too have experienced "night watches." Recently, as I knelt by the sofa in my office in the early morning hours and poured out my anxieties to God, He gently whispered, "Linda, please go to bed. I'll sit up the rest of the night and carry the burden for you. Let Me hold you up in this way." What a picture! The Creator of the universe sits up, waiting, watching, and praying for me, His child, while I sleep. David knew his intimate Friend stayed up and prayed for him.

David boldly declared that God had been his help. Remembering had refreshed his memory and helped him recall what God had done. When we remember, we see proof of the Lord's faithfulness, and this refreshes our hearts and strengthens our confidence in Him. David had made his "I will remember" list! And his mind had then pushed beyond despair to dependence. David's God was a personal God. He called Him *my* God and *my* help. Because David had communion and union with the Holy One, he could follow hard after Him. And my friend, when we experience God's love and are deeply satisfied in Him, when we know Him intimately, we too will cling tightly to Him.

David Had a Desperate Dependence on God

My soul clings to you; your right hand upholds me.
(verse 8)

David possessed two qualities that caused him to cling to his God. He was:

1. Desperate for God.
2. Dependent on God.

Am I desperate for God? Am I dependent on Him? Are you? Tonight I was worshiping with the Michael W. Smith CD *Worship*. One of the songs says:

> *This is the air I breathe*
> *Your holy presence living in me.*
> *This is my daily bread*
> *Your very word spoken to me.*
> *And I, I'm desperate for you.*
> *And I, I'm lost without You.*[3]

We sing the words but do we even begin to know what it means to be desperate and lost without Him?

I Cling to My God

My spirit resonates with David's cry of longing for God. Coming to a desperate dependence on the Holy One has been a long journey for me, but it is a glorious place to be. This once strong, independent child of God called Linda is now weak . . . and in my weakness I am strong. Strongly dependent. Like David, I am learning to cling. The process has not been easy. It has been forged as I've walked through the Valley of Weeping. David was fleeing from Absalom when he wrote Psalm 63. My pain was of a different variety. But pain is pain, and on a desperate, dependent sort of day I composed the following poem based on Psalm 63.

MY SCORCHED SOUL

The hour is late. The shroud of darkness covers the world.
I am shrouded in darkness of another kind.
Pain oozes from a raw wound within my soul.
Deep, searing pain.
It will not go away.
My mind is etched with the streams of this fast flowing pain.
Pain scorches.
Blisters form on the tender curves of my heart.
They pop — sending a flood of fresh anguish over the valleys of my soul.
I ask my Lord,
"Where can I go?"
"What can I do?"
And He answers clearly:
Cling to Me.
I am desperate.
The fingers of my soul stretch — yearn — ache — grasp — cling onto
the Holy One.
He is my lifeline.
I close my eyes and picture myself with pain in hot pursuit.

I jump onto the raft of His presence and cling like a drowning woman.
He upholds me.
My heart awakens to the glorious truth. . . .
Every moment I have been searching, desperate for Him,
He has been holding me in His right hand!
Holding me!
Oh the secure safety to be held by My Father.
Why didn't I know?
Why didn't I feel?
Why did I frantically run in circles of pain when He was always there?
He was always there. Holding me.

I awakened many times the night I wrote "My Scorched Soul," and I remembered my Lord in the night watches. From deep in my spirit, I spoke two words to Him: *I cling.*

I watched my precious friend Becky walk through the valley of breast cancer. I cried with her as her extended family fell apart. At the same time she and her pastor husband had bullets of inter-personal relationship pain coming at them from every direction. I asked Becky, "How do you cling in the midst of continual pain?" She told me that God had given her an image of what clinging looked like for her:

> *God showed me a picture of me as a tiny child with my*
> *arms around the neck of my Savior. We are in the ocean*
> *of life and all around the waves are crashing. A wave*

hits, washing over me. I swallow, choke, and sputter. I
cling tighter. Another wave . . . water and salt burn my
eyes, sending forth fresh tears. I cannot bear to look. The
waves are huge, daunting. I bury my head in His chest.
The rhythm of His heartbeat comforts me and, for a
moment, I am quiet. I lift my head. CRASH! Another
wave pounds me with another rush of salt water. Water
rushes up my nose, in my mouth, in my eyes. I gulp for
breath but find none. My arms slip; I'm too weak to hold
on any longer. Drowning seems inevitable. Then I hear
Him whisper, "I have you, my child. Nestle against My
chest. As you cling to Me remember: I HOLD ON TO
YOU."

God held Becky. God held me. God held David. And — are
you ready for this? God holds *you*! God promises to uphold you
with His righteous right hand.

How does such a promise become real in our lives? God made
this promise real for me by helping me see myself holding on to
Him as my life raft. He gave Becky an image of herself nestled
against God's chest with His arms around her. David saw himself
hiding under the shadow of His wings.

Could it be that you, also, need a personal picture, an intimate image that will encourage you when the storms of life batter
you? If so, lay this book aside for a moment and ask your Father
to show you what clinging looks like for you.

In May 1995 I wrote next to this poem—"I am fenced in but clinging."

> *It puzzles me; but Lord, You understand*
> *And will one day explain this crooked thing.*
> *Meanwhile, I know that it has worked Your best*
> *Its very crookedness taught me to cling.*
>
> *So I will thank and praise You for this puzzle,*
> *And trust where I cannot understand.*
> *Rejoicing You hold me worth such testing,*
> *I cling the closer to Your guiding hand.*[4]

CLING TO GOD'S WORD

David was a clinging man. He stuck like glue to God and to His Word. In Psalm 119:31 (NLT) he wrote, "I cling to your decrees." David grabbed God's Word and held on to it with all his might. In times of distress he clutched the Word and squeezed from it peace and direction. David said God's Word was his food, the very fiber of his being, and the strength of his life.

Why did David cling to God's Word? He gave an abundance of reasons, reasons that can encourage those of us who travel through the Valley of Weeping. David shouts to you and me, "As pressure and stress bear down on me, I find joy in your commands" (Psalm 119:143, NLT). And David found not just joy but help overflowing. The following list taken from Psalm 119 (NLT) fills my heart with hope!

God's Word:

* Keeps me from sin. (verse 11)
* Gives me guidance. (verses 19,98,105)
* Gives me wise advice. (verses 24,98)
* Revives me. (verses 25,50)
* Gives me encouragement. (verse 28)
* Gives me freedom. (verse 45)
* Comforts me in all my troubles. (verses 50,52)
* Restores joy and health. (verse 93)
* Gives me understanding. (verse 104)
* Is my source of hope. (verse 114)
* Fills me with great peace. (verse 165)

My friend Phyllis and I have a covenant to "finish well" together. I asked her how she clings to God's Word.

I read God's Word until He speaks to my heart
— showing me something of His character that I can
praise Him for or draw from or lean on. If I need God's
comfort, I read until God gives comfort. If I need God's

guidance, I read until He challenges me to action. Always God speaks to the needs of my everyday life.

I'll never forget the day that I learned my daughter, Debbie, had diabetes. I was six weeks pregnant and battling morning sickness, but as the doctor explained the prognosis all my attention was focused upon reassuring my frightened seven-year-old. With tears in her eyes she asked, "I won't need shots, will I, Mommy?" Not only would she need shots for the rest of her life, but I would have to learn to give them to her.

The moment I got home I ran to the Lord and to His Word. I did not want to be with anyone or speak to anyone until God spoke to my heart and comforted me. "O God, help me to show my child Your love so that she will never doubt Your goodness. Help me pour out the gift of mercy that does not come naturally for me as I sit by her hospital bed day and night. Give me Your strength, Your love, Your comfort."

As I cried, I read God's Word and it boomed into my heart from Mark 12:11: "This is the Lord's doing, it is an amazing thing to see." And from Psalm 34:18: "The Lord is close to the brokenhearted. He even protects them from accidents." Those verses not only comforted me in that moment, but I prayed them thousands of times in the days that followed.

We adjusted to the diabetes and, for a while, life

was as normal as it could be. But when Debbie was thirteen, she went into a diabetic coma. As she lay in the hospital bed, fear engulfed me as I studied her pristine features. God's Word filled my heart with His presence as I read Isaiah 40:11: "He will feed His flock like a shepherd; He will gather the lambs in His arms, carrying them in His bosom and gently leading those that are with young."[5]

I pictured Jesus holding Debbie in His strong and loving arms; then I pictured Him holding and leading me. When Debbie regained consciousness, I encouraged her to cling to God's Word. I suggested she read John 14 because the Holy Spirit had prompted my heart to recommend that passage. I begged God to do for her what I could not do. Later, she said, "Mom, when I was reading the Bible, it was just like Jesus was comforting me." I cried, knowing exactly how she felt. Oh the joy of feeling His comforting arms around me as I cling to His Word.

As I look back and think about the most challenging moments in my life, almost without fail I can link a Scripture God used to encourage my needy heart to that event. The Lord has shown me that my responsibility is to cling to His Word, and His responsibility — no, His delight — is to comfort me.

WILL YOU CLING?

God desires that we grow in learning to cling to Him and to His Word. I have asked God to create in me a "desperate dependence" so that I will cling tightly to Him. The Valley of Weeping has been my schoolroom. I thank God for every step in the valley because I am learning to cling like a child. If you are in the Valley of Weeping, you are also in the School of Learning to Cling. This is reason for rejoicing! Out of your deep pain can come a woman who clings to her God and to His Word.

The story is told of a group of botanists who searched the Alps for rare specimens of flowers. On a precipitous ledge in a steep canyon they spied a rare flower they had been searching many years to find. The botanists offered a passing shepherd boy a large sum of money if he would allow them to tie a lifeline around his waist, lower him down to where the flower was, and retrieve it.

The boy considered all he could do with the money, but then peered down into the deep cavern, and shook his head "no." He desperately wanted the money, but the cliff was unbelievably dangerous and these men were strangers—how could he trust them with his life? Again and again he looked at the canyon and the prized money but continued to shake his head. But then he had an idea . . . a good idea. He ran across the mountainside, entered a house, and emerged with a strong, kindly man—his father. Clinging to his father's hand, he raced back to the group of men waiting at the edge of the cliff, and said, "You may tie the lifeline under my arms now. I will go down into the canyon — *if* you let my father hold the rope."[6]

Tied to his father, the boy felt safe. And tied to your Father, you are safe!

Will you cling to your God? The Father will hold you up and carry you when you can't walk.

Will you cling to God's Word? The Spirit of the Living God will use the Word to revive and encourage you.

Do you hear the voice of the Holy Spirit speaking personally to you? He is saying,

> *As you cling, I, who am in you, will take the promise to revive you and pour refreshment, renewal, and restoration into your scorched soul. As you cling, I, the Spirit, whose name is Encouragement, will pour courage into you to face this problem.*

The Song of Holy Pilgrimage

How lovely is your dwelling place,

O LORD Almighty!

My soul yearns, even faints,

or the courts of the LORD;

my heart and my flesh cry out

for the living God.

Even the sparrow has found a

home,

and the swallow a nest for herself,

where she may have her young —

a place near your altar,

O LORD Almighty, my King and

my God.

Blessed are those who dwell in your

house;

they are ever praising you.

Blessed are those whose strength is

in you,

who have set their hearts on

pilgrimage.

As they pass through the Valley of

Weeping,

they make it a place of springs;

the autumn rains also cover it with

pools.

They go from strength to strength,

till each appears before God in

Zion.

Hear my prayer, O LORD God

Almighty;

listen to me, O God of Jacob.

Look upon our shield, O God;

look with favor on your anointed

one.

Better is one day in your courts

than a thousand elsewhere;

I would rather be a doorkeeper in

the house of my God

than dwell in the tents of the

wicked.

For the LORD God is a sun and

shield;

The LORD bestows favor and

honor;

no good thing does he withhold

from those whose walk is blameless.

O LORD Almighty,

blessed is the man who trusts in

you.

PSALM 84

Chapter Five

I Journey

SOME JOURNEYS ARE BY PLANE

Airplanes and I are good friends. This past year I've flown to Hungary, Ukraine, and England, as well as many places across the United States.

My husband and I react very differently to being on a plane for more than a day. After eating dinner and enjoying a movie, he positions his neck pillow, puts on his eye covers, and settles in to his snoring routine, out for the count. I, on the other hand, do not sleep. I can't sleep because I just can't sleep. And I can't sleep because I have to stay awake to do my job—poke the snoring, snorting, wheezing man next to me so he doesn't disrupt the entire plane. I once surprised myself by falling asleep on the never-ending flight to Asia, but on awakening I felt so dizzy I fainted. Believe me, the huge oxygen tank and mask the flight attendant strapped on me were *not* worth the fifteen minutes of sleep!

Even though air travel sometimes includes oxygen masks and snoring husbands, I love to fly because it is a "perspective giver." Soaring high above the scattered clouds, I am given a unique panoramic view of the heavens and the earth.

Some journeys are by foot

Each spring I anticipate the day the winter snows melt and I can once again go on my "holy hike" to the waterfall hidden high in the mountains behind my home. One May day the weatherman called for dense fog, but the skies looked clear so I headed up the path to my waterfall. The trek up was magnificent. Majestic pine trees and multicolored wildflowers danced in the wind, delighting my senses. The climb over huge boulders that blocked the entrance to my waterfall caused this over sixty-year-old body to huff and puff. But the treasure of my hiding place was worth the effort.

After spending time in quiet reflection and wonder, dwelling in God's presence, I started back but quickly discovered that the weatherman's prediction had been accurate after all. Thick pea-soup fog had cascaded over the mountain, shrouding the world in gray gloom and completely obscuring my way.

Traveling by foot is delightful on sun-filled days, but becomes dreary and even fear-filled when fog clouds our vision. Then we can barely see the path at our feet, let alone what's up around the bend.

Some Christians hope their spiritual journey will be like traveling on a 747 jumbo jet on a calm day with no turbulence. The trip may even get boring—but a nice kind of boring. We like the idea of reclining our seat, reading a good novel, and being served the drink of our choice.

While our walk with God *is* a journey, any hopes for a jumbo jet ride will remain just that—hopes. You and I are pilgrims on the path that God has set before us. Sometimes we walk through lush green forests and dancing wildflowers. Other times we travel through Valleys of Weeping, groping our way through thick fog.

Christians throughout the centuries have pictured the walk of faith as a pilgrimage. John Bunyan, in *The Pilgrim's Progress*, described each stage of the journey as "fog-filled." Teresa of Avila, in *The Interior Castle*, pictured a Christian traveling through a progression of mansions toward the center of the castle where His Majesty dwelled. Hannah Hurnard, in *Hinds' Feet on High Places*, depicted little Much-Afraid as longing to journey to the dwelling place of God with Joy and Comfort as her companions. The Shepherd's choice was not Joy and Comfort but Sorrow and Suffering. Each of these classic works had an ultimate destination—God's presence. Yet in each book, the sojourners discovered that the journey itself—*and who they became while passing through the Valleys of*

Weeping—was of utmost importance.

The message is the same in Psalm 84. It is about one who journeys with her eyes focused on the ultimate destination—*the presence of God*—and the blessings of character that are developed as she walks by faith. Come with me and learn from the Song of Holy Pilgrimage how you too can know the blessing of His presence and become "a blessed one."

THE SONG OF HOLY PILGRIMAGE

Psalm 84 is a psalm of pilgrimage. I define *pilgrimage* as a journey to a sacred place, and in this psalm that sacred place is the presence of God. The psalmist did not make his pilgrimage by plane . . . probably not even by camel. He walked—and obviously encountered many foggy days. Physically, his destination was Jerusalem and the "courts of the Lord," but we misunderstand if we limit this poem to a literal interpretation. The "courts of the Lord" also represent God's presence. The pilgrim's journey was not just to a place, but to a Person. His ultimate destination was the presence of God.[1]

This psalmist celebrates the blessedness of intimate communion with God (verses 1-7) and prays that he may enter into the glorious presence of the Holy One (verses 8-12). While many commentators believe this psalm to have been written by the Sons of Korah, others believe David wrote it. The passion and longing for God is reminiscent of Psalm 63, the Song of Holy Clinging, so I too believe David wrote it. (It helps that Charles Spurgeon wrote, "Psalm 84 exhales to us a Davidic perfume."[2])

Hidden in this precious Song of Holy Pilgrimage is the blessing we receive as we journey to God's presence:

- The Valley of Weeping *can* become a Place of Blessing!
- The one who journeys *can* be blessed!
- The presence of God *can* become real!

First, let's look at how God's presence was real to the psalmist.

THE DWELLING PLACE

More than anything else, the psalmist wanted to abide in the dwelling place of God's presence. We vividly see his passion for God in the first verses:

> *How lovely is your dwelling place, O LORD Almighty!*
> *My soul yearns, even faints, for the courts of the LORD;*
> *my heart and my flesh cry out for the living God.*
> *(verses 1-2)*

These passionate words beautifully demonstrate the author's love relationship with the Living God. What are your thoughts when you read these emotional words of intimate longing? I think we often breeze right past them — they are just too emotion-packed, or we assume the psalm must be talking about heaven and the joy we will experience there. Not so. The psalmist is talking about a place in which we can dwell right now. He experienced the fullness of joy in God's presence *in the present* (see Psalm 16:11). My friend, do you see? We can experience the joy of His presence right now . . . *today!*

Perhaps, like me, you have looked at a woman who had a deep love relationship with the Lord and asked, "God, what's wrong with me? Is this just not for me?" I can remember reading these verses about God's dwelling place and thinking, *I just cannot relate . . . does anyone really have this yearning, fainting, flesh-crying-out passion for God?* I wasn't sure I knew anyone who literally panted after God—but somewhere deep in my spirit I longed to know and experience this place of God's presence.

This place is so lovely, so beautiful, that the psalmist desperately yearned to go there. To him, one day in the presence of the Lord was so wonderful that one thousand days of earthly delight could not compare. He thirsted so intensely for God's presence that he even offered to become a janitor in His courts—*anything* to dwell in the lovely place of His presence (see Psalm 84:10).

Many years after the fire of longing for God's presence first sparked in my heart, I met women whose faces radiated a deep joy and whose hearts remained calm in the midst of chaos. They spoke of God with passion and intimacy. I wanted what they had! My heart cried, "Take me deeper, Holy Spirit; take me deeper into all You are, all the Son is, and all the Father is. I long to abide in the presence of the Holy One." And in time God began to draw me to the glorious place of His presence. A place of joy.

A place of comfort. A place of deep intimacy. A place of passion. A place of peace . . . even in the Valley of Weeping.

Most Christians know that God is everywhere, omnipresent. But many do not understand that He can envelop each of us with His personal presence. It is difficult to describe what this is like—God manifests Himself differently to each person. And only God knows His personal plans for you and His timing for your life. I have a dear friend who has walked for four years through a deep Valley of Weeping, and during this time God has seemed silent and distant. She has longed for His presence, and I know He will give her the desire of her heart—in His timing. I cannot tell you *how* or *when* He will manifest Himself in your life. What I can promise you is this: He longs for you to know His presence. Why don't you put down this book and ask Him right now to reveal His presence to you? You could pray something like this:

> *O my God, I long to know this yearning, fainting,*
> *flesh-crying-out passion. I don't know where to begin . . .*
> *please take me deeper. I long to experience Your presence.*

When we experience God's manifest presence, we are changed.

The Names of God

In the early years of my Christian walk, I called God Father and Lord, for I knew God to be these things. But now that I have come to dwell in His presence, I use more intimate and personal names: My Holy One; My Father; My Bridegroom; Gracious Lord; My Sovereign King; the High and Lifted Up One; My Magnificent, Majestic God. No name seems *enough* to declare all that He is.

The way we address God reveals much about our relationship with Him. In Psalm 84 the psalmist seems to search his heart for new ways to declare the glory of the Holy One. "God" and "Lord" alone do not express the deep emotion in his heart.

The psalmist addressed God as "O Lord Almighty, the living God." As the psalm progresses, he declared God to be: "my King," the "God of Jacob," the "Lord God," and his "sun and shield." Four times he addressed God as "O Lord Almighty." Four times in twelve verses! It is as if the writer shouted, "I have no words to express Your beauty, Your grandeur, so I will put several words together in an effort to express the glory of my God."

This kind of repetition in the Word of God tells my spiritual ears, "The name *O Lord Almighty* is important." The Hebrew word translated "Almighty" means "God of Hosts or Armies."[3] This is why *The Message* renders the name of God "O Lord Almighty" as "God of the Angel Armies"! God commands the angelic forces of heaven. He is Lord of the Armies. He is a living, active God—active in the great wars of history but also in the personal wars I encounter here on earth.

My blessing as I journey through the Valley of Weeping is dwelling in the presence of my mighty, yet personal, God.

The Blessed One

As we progress through Psalm 84, we see another wonderful truth: As the blessing of His presence becomes mine, I can become "a blessed one."

Three times the writer of this psalm used the Hebrew word *barak*, which is translated *bless*[4] and means "to endue with power for success."[5] What an encouragement! When my pilgrimage includes fog-filled valleys, I am tempted to give up—to sit down and sob. I need power to keep on walking.

A "blessed one" possesses qualities that bring blessing, qualities that say, "This woman trusts and obeys the Lord." To this kind of woman, God gives His richest, most abundant life and the secret place of His presence.

Are you thinking what I think you are thinking? *Linda, if blessing means I'm given a rich and abundant life, I'm not among the blessed. My life is a Valley of Weeping, not a mountaintop of blessing.* If these are your thoughts, you are in good company! The psalmists we've looked at in this book also questioned why life was so filled with problems, pain, and perplexities.

Look carefully at one of the qualities of a "blessed one." "Blessed is [the one] whose help is the God of Jacob, whose hope is in the Lord" (Psalm 146:5, NASB). This indicates that this person was not on a mountaintop, but in a valley. In the valleys we need help and hope! In the valleys we grow in becoming a "blessed one."

Look with me at the three "blessed" statements in Psalm 84, and you will see that the "blessed one" is rich and her life abundant, *not* because the path of her life is smooth but because she walks the path enveloped by God's presence.

Three Attributes of the Blessed One

Because, like the psalmist, the blessed woman has set her heart on entering into His presence, three qualities gradually begin to characterize her. She is a woman of praise, strength, and trust.

A Woman of Praise

> *Blessed are those who dwell in your house; they are ever praising you. (verse 4)*

When we dwell in God's presence, we will praise Him. David praised God seven times every day (see Psalm 119:164). *Halal*[6] is the Hebrew word for *praise* in Psalm 84. *Halal* plus *jah*, an abbreviated form of *Yahweh*, forms the word *hallelujah*, which means "Praise the Lord!" The woman who dwells in the presence of God is always shouting, "Hallelujah!" Even when walking through the Valley of Weeping, words of praise flow from her lips.

Does praising God in a prison of tragic or horrifying circumstances sound impossible? Believe me, it's not. Listen to Beth's words:

> *My journey of holy pilgrimage started with deep unraveling of my soul. When the Holy Spirit began unlocking*

the secret chambers of my mind, I entered the Valley of Weeping. As the Spirit of Truth unlocked closet after closet of horrible memories of sexual abuse, the life I had been so sure of splintered.

In the darkness God graciously brought to me an angel of His mercy, someone who would become to me, "Jesus with skin." God graciously knit my wounded soul into Linda's heart. Her tenderness and love wrapped arms around my broken heart. In gracious tenderness she offered me a challenge that changed my life. Would I be willing to spend the first twenty minutes of each day on my knees in worship, praising God not for what He had allowed but for His holy character? I accepted her challenge and began using worship music to prompt my early morning praise. Sometimes I turned off the music and waited quietly before the Lord, listening for His voice. Other times I would personalize Scripture and pray it back to the Lord, continually asking the Holy Spirit to bring my heart into perfect union with His.

As I knelt by my couch I offered the Almighty praise for all that I knew to be true about His character. "O Lord, I praise You, for You are Almighty. O My Father, I praise You that You are holy and pure. O precious Jesus, I worship You because You love me completely." There on my knees, weeping on my couch, my Valley of Weeping became a Place of Blessing, because in the

horror of darkness the One who is Eternal Light gave
me Himself.

Beth is becoming a blessed one.

Are you growing in becoming a blessed woman of praise?

A Woman of Strength

Blessed are those whose strength is in you, who have set
their hearts on pilgrimage. As they pass through the
Valley of Weeping, they make it a place of springs; the
autumn rains also cover it with pools. They go from
strength to strength, till each appears before God in
Zion. (verses 5-7)

Here we see the promise of Psalm 84. God says He will give us the strength to turn our Valleys of Weeping into a Place of Blessing. What an incredible promise! And to whom does God promise this strength? To the woman who sets her heart on a pilgrimage to the dwelling place of God's presence.

Perhaps your Bible says "Valley of Baca" instead of "Valley of Weeping." Baca is not a specific place, but a reference either to a place of weeping or a valley of desolation. It means "the pilgrim turns his troubles into blessings."[7] The woman of strength dares to dig blessings out of hardships.

A blessed one has made a secret choice. She has said, "I want to dwell in the presence of God. I set my heart on knowing Him—whatever it costs, wherever the journey leads. I want to walk worthily through the Valley of Weeping. I fix my heart on honoring my God and discovering the joy and passion the psalmist knew."

This woman is blessed. In her weakness, God becomes her strength, and when she passes through a Valley of Weeping her strength increases. She personally discovers that God always gives His people the supplies they need while traveling the road that He appoints.

Andrea hated the road she was traveling, but she had set her heart to know God in the midst of her Valley of Weeping:

> *I told a friend that when I learned about my husband's involvement in pornography, I felt like I'd been catapulted into the middle of a desert. It was a horrible place. All I did was cry. But as I began to try to find my way out of the desert wasteland, I saw that there are some good things about being in the desert. For one, I had to depend totally on God. And I realized that when I see glimpses of beauty in the desert, it is a glorious gift because most of what I see is dry and empty.*
>
> *It is good for me to think about the "positives" of life in the desert whenever I walk out of one of those beauty spots into the barren desert again. Never would I have imagined that my Christian husband would struggle*

with this sin. But I want to know God's presence in the
midst of this horrible pain.

Andrea has "set her heart on pilgrimage," and she is becoming a woman of strength. Have you set your heart? Are you becoming a woman whose strength is in God?

A Woman of Trust

Blessed is the [woman] who trusts in you. (verse 12)

The blessed woman lives out the biblical definition of faith found in Hebrews 11:1: "Faith is the assurance of things hoped for, the conviction of things *not seen*" (NASB, emphasis added). Faith is holding God's hand as you walk through the fog. When you can't see, when you don't understand because fog blurs your vision, look beyond the fog to the Expert in Fog Removal. Make a secret choice to trust God's way.

This story from the Battle of Waterloo in 1815 gives us a picture of looking beyond the fog:

It was a critical time for the British Empire. Napoleon's
armies had decimated and conquered Europe. Now the
Emperor, Napoleon, had set his sights on England. To
meet this threat to the homeland, the British sent out
the capable General Wellington to engage the Emperor's

army across the English Channel in France at Waterloo.

England's future rested in the outcome of this battle and the country waited in hopeful agony for word of victory. A system of signal flares was set up all over the country. As soon as the battle had been decided, the signal of victory or defeat was to be flashed across the English Channel and read by a signal post atop the White Cliffs of Dover. Then the signal was to be relayed to another post several miles away, and then to another, and another, until all England heard the news.

As the two armies clashed at Waterloo, England waited with trepidation. Was this to be the end of their beloved homeland or would Wellington defeat Napoleon?

Finally the first messages were flashed across the English Channel:

Wellington defeated.

Then a dense fog rolled across the channel. As the terrifying message was relayed all over the British Isles, a sense of despair gripped the land. England was gone. At any moment they expected the invasion of Napoleon's armies to come storming across the channel.

But then the fog lifted and the complete story was flashed across the channel:

Wellington defeated THE ENEMY!

England had been saved![8]

Like England during the Battle of Waterloo, you and I stand on the other side of the fog. As we journey through the Valley of Weeping, we cannot see the entire picture. As Jesus prayed in the Garden of Gethsemane, it appeared that His life would end in ignominious defeat and terrible torture. Yet, there was more to the story, more than our Savior could see as He wept alone that night. The victory of the Resurrection was only three days away!

It is the same with us. On this side of eternity, all symphonies are unfinished, all stories are incomplete. We see only the events surrounding us. Our myopic vision keeps us from seeing "the other side of the story," the conclusion that we will not understand until we see Him face to face.

But can a woman living in a fog-filled situation in the twenty-first century really trust God for what she can't see? Yes, definitely yes!

My friend, are you trusting God for what you can't see?

CAN PAIN BE A BLESSING?

If I say to the Holy One, "I trust Your ways, I trust Your timing," will He protect me from pain? Of course not. My valleys have been pain-filled, yet I thank my Shepherd for leading me through these Places of Weeping. My "valley time" has produced good things in my life.

Perhaps you are saying, "Right, Linda. Pain is good?" I didn't say I liked the pain, but I rejoice because my heart and will have been transformed in the Valley of Weeping.

How has my *heart* changed?
God's presence is my daily portion.

* I hear His voice.
* I know His touch.
* I sense His presence.

How has my *will* changed?
Trusting God is my daily portion.

* I trust His way.
* I trust His timing.
* I set my will with a deeper resolve.

Often we have heard it said, "no pain, no gain." We repeat these words to our children when they are ready to quit the track team because running laps is too hard. I say it to myself when working out at the gym sounds as exciting as eating rubber. This phrase applies not only in the realm of athletics but also to the spiritual realm. The pattern we see in the Lord Jesus' earthly pilgrimage bears this out. God uses suffering to bring glory to Himself and His Son.

It causes me pain to think of my Savior in such agony that drops of blood poured from His body. I grieve when I watch those I love drip emotional "drops of blood." Suffering is the last thing I consider useful, but as I look back over my life, I see

it has been God's most effective tool "to grow me up in Him."
Why? Because nothing highlights my need for God like a valley
of affliction. When I feel weak, weary, and worried, *I remember
the deeds of God. I hide in His refuge. I cling in desperate dependence. I walk in faith.* And these secret choices bring Him great
glory!

I began this book by talking about how my heart was broken
over the pain of God's women. As I watched my friends walk
through deep, seemingly endless valleys, I told God, "The pain is
too much." And He gently whispered to me, "Linda, I promised
that no valley would be so deep that I would not be deeper still.
I promised that with the valley I would provide a way of escape
(see 1 Corinthians 10:13). I will send the escape route for those
you love . . . and for you."

Corrie ten Boom discovered the transforming power of
suffering in a Nazi concentration camp as she watched her
beloved sister, Betsy, die of starvation and illness. She also saw
her friends gassed and burned in the ovens of the camp. Corrie's
life speaks to us from a place of death. Corrie, who knew the
Valley of Weeping in ways that we cannot even imagine, said her
Great God was in the midst of the horror, holding her, encour-
aging her. And who was the woman who emerged from this
deep, deep suffering? Corrie was a woman who praised God.
A woman whose strength was in God. A woman whose middle
name was Trust. Corrie ten Boom had "faithful feet." So did
Enoch.

FAITHFUL FEET

Enoch faithfully *walked* with God for 365 years—a *very* long journey. I'm sure some days his feet skipped through lush forest glades where a waterfall of health and happiness poured over him. But on other days, he passed through Valleys of Weeping, where his feet stumbled over stony, hard, dry places and his only food was sorrow and suffering. Yet over every mountaintop, through every valley, Enoch kept walking. His focus was fixed on the One he loved, and he faithfully put one foot in front of the other and walked.

God gives an unusual tribute to Enoch. On his tombstone God wrote four simple words: "Enoch walked with Me." And his walk of faith so delighted God's heart that "Enoch was not because God took him."[9] Enoch had faithful feet.

The Christian life is not the one hundred-meter dash. It is more like a twenty-six mile marathon, and I am a participant in this race of life called the "Glory of God." I've signed up, donned my T-shirt with a "Glory to God" logo on the back, and now I am in the long, slow race—headed toward the goal of glorifying the Most Holy One with every step I take.

Charles Stanley says that to glorify something is to arrange things so as to focus attention on it or bring it honor. We glorify a picture when we hang it at a focal point in a room. We add further glory to it by shining a light on it.[10] And, my friend, we glorify God when we look beyond the fog and trust Him in the midst of the valley. It is as if God shines a light through us—

people watch and hearts are turned to the Holy One because we walk at peace through the valley of pain.

This book began with three questions:

1. Is it possible to go through the Valley of Weeping without falling apart?
2. Is it possible to have joy in the midst of suffering?
3. Is it possible to grow in intimacy with the Lord as we travel through the valley?

God and the psalmists say, "Yes," and I say, "Yes."

I pray you also can now say, "*Yes!*"

It is true! It is really true! As I have passed through the Valley of Weeping, God has made it a Place of Blessing! There is a spring flowing over the barren soil of my heart. And joy of joys,

- I am blessed — not because life is easy, but because I abide in the dwelling place of God's presence.
- I am blessed — not because heartache and trials have vanished, but because God has changed me from a servant to a worshiper.
- I am blessed — not because I have become strong, but because He is becoming my strength.
- I am blessed — not because I can see the way and timing of God, but because He is becoming my total trust.

And, my friend, do you know that as you pass through the Valley of Weeping you do not walk alone? Jesus said, "It is better that I leave because *then* the Holy Spirit, the Journey-Mate I have given you, can come." He will walk ahead of you, forming the footprints when the valley is deep. He will walk behind you, praying that the steep path and rocks strewn in your path will not cause you to stumble. He will continually lift your weary heart to the Father who loves you and pray for you with groans too deep for words. And when the pain of the Valley of Weeping seems too much to bear, the Comforter who ever journeys with you will gently pick you up in His arms and carry you. Your footprints then become one with His.

As the Encourager carries you, He will breathe new hope into you. His voice will be clear:

> *Remember,*
> > *hide,*
> > > *cling,*
> > > > *journey.*

Keep walking.

Look up! You will dwell in the presence of God!
Look up! You will become a woman of praise!
Look up! You will become a woman of strength!
Look up! You will become a woman of trust!
Look up! You will know a deeper kind of calm!

Bible Study

Dear Friend,

I'm excited about what God is going to do in your life as a
result of your choice to do this study. I pray that the Holy One
will encourage your heart as you study His Word. May He give
you hope as you walk through the Valley of Weeping and show
you how it can become a Place of Blessing.

Bible study is good, but *memorizing* and *meditating* on
God's Word are the best ways to place His Word in your heart
and mind. Cynthia Heald has said that memorizing Scripture
increases the Holy Spirit's vocabulary in your life.[1] For this
reason, each of these four lessons includes verses to memorize.
As we lay up God's Word and wisdom in our hearts, we will be
changed.

You can do this four-week Bible study in a group, with a
friend, or by yourself. My prayer for you is that at the end of the

four weeks, you will see God in a new way and be able to say, "As I walk through this Valley of Weeping, I am learning to *Remember*, *Hide*, *Cling*, and *Journey*, and I see God's Blessing to me!"

I will be praying for you as you learn from Him!

LINDA DILLOW

Week One

1. Read chapter 1, "My Valley of Weeping," and chapter 2, "I Remember," at least once.

2. Memorize Psalm 77:11-12 as written here from the NIV or in another translation.

> *I will remember the deeds of the LORD;*
> *yes, I will remember your miracles of long ago.*
> *I will meditate on all your works*
> *and consider all your mighty deeds.*

3. Read Psalm 77 three times and meditate on the message.

    a. What is the overall theme of the psalm?

    b. Write three statements that stand out to you from the psalm.

4. Paraphrase Psalm 77:1-8 and write it here.

5. In Psalm 77:6 Asaph tried to remember but his despair continued. How was his "remembering" in verses 11 and following different from his "remembering" in verse 6?

6. Describe your own Valley of Weeping.

7. Asaph said, "I will remember."

   a. Spend a half hour alone with God at some point this
       week. Ask Him to bring to mind His deeds, His miracles,
       His works, and His mighty acts to *you* in *your* personal
       history. Then write your "I Remember" list.

   b. Read your "I Remember" list out loud and then answer
       this question: If you see *who* God is and *what* He has
       done in the history of your personal life, can you trust
       Him *now* in your Valley of Weeping? Write a prayer to
       the Lord expressing how you desire to trust Him.

8. Read Deuteronomy 8:11-14.

    a. List the things in this passage that cause us to forget what God has done.

    b. Make a list of the things that cause you to forget.

9. Deuteronomy 8:2 (NASB) says, "And you shall remember
    all the way which the LORD your God has led you in the
    wilderness." To help you grow in "remembering," consider
    beginning a Wilderness Journal where you weekly record
    your experience of God's wonders, works, and mighty deeds
    as you walk through this Valley of Weeping. In years to
    come, this record will encourage you to trust Him.

10. What did you learn about God this week? What did you
    learn about yourself? Write a prayer to remember what God
    has taught you.

Week Two

1. Read chapter 3, "I Hide," at least once.

2. Memorize these two verses from Psalm 46 as written here from the NIV or in another translation.

God is our refuge and strength,
an ever-present help in trouble.
(verse 1)

Be still, and know that I am God;
I will be exalted among the nations,
I will be exalted in the earth.
(verse 10)

3. Read Psalm 46 thoughtfully three times.

    a. Why do you think this psalm has been known for centuries as "The Song of Holy Confidence"?

    b. List at least five reasons this psalm encourages your heart.

    c. Is there anything in the psalm that brings you discouragement?

4. Describe a time when you experienced God as your refuge.

5. Read Psalms 3:3; 18:2; and 27:5. God desires that we use our minds to direct our hearts to the safety of the hiding place of His refuge. Write a description of how you do this.

6. The message of Psalm 46 is that no matter what storm sweeps across our lives, we can hide in the secret refuge of His presence.

    a. Where do you think Christian women hide during a Valley of Weeping?

    b. Make a list of where you run for refuge. Is it to a person, a place, or a thing?

7. My friend Mimi cried out in prayer to God (see page 49).
    Write a prayer in which you cry out to God for help with
    the problem you are facing now.

8. God commands us to "Be still" so we can know He is God.
    Keep track of the minutes of silence and solitude you have
    this week. How can you create time in your busy life to "be
    still"? Outline your plan here.

9. Write a letter or an e-mail to a friend in pain. Using what you have learned from Psalm 46, encourage your friend that God will be her refuge, help, and fortress.

10. What did you learn about God this week? What did you learn about yourself? Write a prayer to remember what God has taught you.

Week Three

1. Read chapter 4, "I Cling," at least once.

2. Memorize Psalm 63:1 or 63:8 (or both!) as written here from the NIV or in another translation.

O God, you are my God,
earnestly I seek you;
my soul thirsts for you,
my body longs for you,
in a dry and weary land
where there is no water.
(verse 1)
My soul clings to you;
your right hand upholds me.
(verse 8)

WE ARE TO CLING TO GOD

3. Read Psalm 63 thoughtfully three times. Can you remember
    a time when you experienced "clinging"? (A time when a
    toddler or dress clung to you, or when you physically clung
    to something?) Describe your feelings.

4. Meditate on Psalm 63:1-2. David longed for God.

    a. What thoughts come to your mind when you read, "My
        soul thirsts for you, my body longs for you"?

b. How can you develop a "hungering" and "thirsting" after God?

5. Meditate on Psalm 63:3-6. David found satisfaction with God.

a. Describe what your mind dwells on when you experience "night watches."

b. What would encourage you to shift your "night watch" thoughts to God and His protective care of you?

6. Meditate on Psalm 63:6-8. David had an intimate friendship with God.

a. Write a paragraph or poem describing what "desperate dependence" looks like to you.

b. How can you move toward making the words of Michael W. Smith's song (page 70) a reality in your life?

7. Reread the poem "My Scorched Soul" on pages 71-72 and Becky's description of clinging on pages 72-73. Do you have a personal picture of what spiritual clinging looks and feels like for you? Describe it here.

We Are to Cling to God's Word

8. Read Psalm 119. This psalm has only one theme, the Word of God. David said, "As pressure and stress bear down on me, I find joy in your commands" (Psalm 119:143, NLT).

   a. Reread the list taken from Psalm 119 that filled David's heart with hope (page 75). Pick at least three promises from this list and describe how each promise gives you hope in your Valley of Weeping.

   b. As you look back at your life, can you remember times when God has spoken to you through His Word? Describe a time and the Scripture God gave to encourage you.

9. What did you learn about God this week? What did you learn about yourself? Write a prayer to God to express what you learned.

Week Four

1. Read chapter 5, "I Journey," at least once.

2. Memorize Psalm 84:5-7 as written here from the NIV or in another translation.

> *Blessed are those whose strength is in you,*
> *who have set their hearts on pilgrimage.*
> *As they pass through the Valley of Weeping,*
> *they make it a place of springs. . . .*
> *They go from strength to strength,*
> *till each appears before God in Zion.*

3. Read Psalm 84 thoughtfully three times. Meditate on Psalm 84:1-2. Write a paragraph describing your thoughts and feelings as you read these words of longing for the presence of God.

4. Psalm 84:4 says, "Blessed are those who dwell in your house; they are ever praising you." Reread the section about praising God and Beth's testimony (pages 92-94). I challenged Beth to take "The 20-Minute Worship Challenge." This week I encourage you to do the same. Spend 10-20 minutes every day before the Lord in worship. At the end of the week record here anything you learned about becoming a woman of praise.

5. Read Hebrews 11, "The Faith Hall of Fame." Then reread the section "A Woman of Trust" and the story of the Battle of Waterloo (pages 96-98).

    a. List at least five things you see in the Scripture and story about faith.

    b. How can you become a "blessed woman who trusts" as you walk through your Valley of Weeping?

6. I said that my pain has been a blessing. Ask God to reveal to you ways He has used pain in your life. Write at least three here.

7. Read Genesis 5:21-24. Enoch had "faithful feet." Write a prayer to God telling Him what it looks like for you to lift your eyes beyond the fog and have "faithful feet."

8. How has your view of God changed during this four-week study?

9. List five things that God has taught you during these four weeks as you've studied the Psalms and learned about *remembering, hiding, clinging,* and *journeying.*

10. How has God given you hope that your Valley of Weeping can become a Place of Blessing?

Notes

CHAPTER 2

1. Charles Haddon Spurgeon, *The Treasury of David, Vol. 2* (Grand Rapids, Mich.: Zondervan, 1966), 313.

2. Paul Lee Tan, *7,700 Illustrations* (Rockville, Md.: Assurance Publishers, 1979), 1513.

3. I received this story over the Internet. I have done a Google search and have been unable to find a reference to the story.

CHAPTER 3

1. Elisabeth Elliott, *Facing the Death of Someone You Love* (Westchester, Ill.: Good News, 1980), 8.

2. Cf. Deuteronomy 32:37; 2 Samuel 22:3; Psalm 91:2; Nahum 1:7; and so on.

3. Bob Sorge, *Secrets of the Secret Place* (Lees Summit, Mo.: Oasis House, 2001), 29.

CHAPTER 4

1. Charles Haddon Spurgeon, *The Treasury of David*, updated by Roy H. Clarke (Nashville: Thomas Nelson, 1997), 522.

2. Charles Haddon Spurgeon, *The Treasury of David, Vol. 2* (Grand Rapids, Mich.: Zondervan, 1966), 66.

3. Used by permission.

4. Mrs. Charles E. Cowman, *Streams in the Desert, Vol. 1*, adapted (Grand Rapids, Mich.: Zondervan, 1925), 77.

5. All Scriptures in this excerpt are paraphrases.

6. Mrs. Charles E. Cowman, *Streams in the Desert, Vol. 2*, adapted (Grand Rapids, Mich.: Zondervan, 1966), 68.

CHAPTER 5

1. James Montgomery Boice, *Psalms, Vol. 2* (Grand Rapids, Mich.: Baker, 1996), 692-693.

2. Charles Haddon Spurgeon, *The Treasury of David, Vol. 2* (Grand Rapids, Mich.: Zondervan, 1966), 432.

3. Lawrence O. Richards, *Expository Dictionary of Bible Words* (Grand Rapids, Mich.: Zondervan, 1985), 33.

4. R. Laird Harris, ed., *Theological Wordbook of the Old Testament* (Chicago: Moody, 1980), 1:132.

5. Richards, 130.

6. R. L. Harris, G. L. Archer, and B. K. Waltke, *Theological Wordbook of the Old Testament* (Chicago: Moody, 1980, 1999 electronic edition).

7. *Ryrie Study Bible, New American Standard Bible* version. Note on Psalm 84:6.

8. Andre Bernard and Clifton Fadiman, *Bartlett's Book of Anecdotes* (Boston: Little, Brown, revised ed. 2000). This incident is also depicted in Alfred Werker's 1934 film *House of Rothschild.*

9. Adapted from Genesis 5:21-24.

10. Charles Stanley, *How to Handle Adversity* (Nashville: Nelson, 1989), 36.

BIBLE STUDY

1. From a message given at a women's retreat, Tri-Lakes Chapel, Monument, Colorado, April 1995.

Recommended Reading

A Deeper Kind of Calm is about how to seek God in the midst of Valleys of Weeping. It does not deal with the question of why God allows the valleys in our lives. For help with that question, I refer you to the following books:

Dobson, Dr. James. *When God Doesn't Make Sense.* Tyndale, 2001.

Eareckson Tada, Joni. *When God Weeps.* Zondervan, 2000.

Morrissey, Kirkie. *God, Where Are You?* NavPress, 2002.

Nelson, Alan. *Embracing Brokenness.* NavPress, 2002.

Yancey, Philip. *Disappointment with God.* Zondervan, 1997.

Yancey, Philip. *Where Is God When It Hurts?* Zondervan, 1997.

About the Author

LINDA DILLOW and her husband, Jody, lived in Europe and Asia for seventeen years training Christian leaders in closed countries with Biblical Education by Extension (BEE). During that time, Linda traveled extensively in Romania, Russia, Hungary, Poland, and Asia teaching and mentoring women. Linda speaks at women's retreats, Intimate Issues Conferences, and also in Asia and Europe.

Her books include *Calm My Anxious Heart* and *Creative Counterpart*. She has coauthored *Intimate Issues* and *Intimacy Ignited*.

The Dillows live in Monument, Colorado. They have four grown children and seven grandchildren.

GROW IN CONTENTMENT AND FAITH.

Calm My Anxious Heart

Linda Dillow

1-57683-047-0

If you're tired of worrying about all the "what-ifs" in your life and want to experience the calm and contentment promised in Scripture, *Calm My Anxious Heart* is what you've been looking for. Filled with encouragement and practical help for overcoming anxiety, this book includes a twelve-week Bible study to help you discover what the Bible says about contentment and ways to apply it to your daily life.

Calm My Anxious Heart: My Mercies Journal

Linda Dillow

1-57683-116-7

The companion journal to *Calm My Anxious Heart* will help you focus on growing in contentment and faith as you learn to trust God completely.